GARFIELD

I Don't Do Windows!

JIM DAVIS

D0237657

RAVETTE PUBLISHING

© 2013 PAWS, INCORPORATED
All rights reserved.

"GARFIELD" and the GARFIELD characters
are trademarks of Paws, Incorporated.

(www.garfield.com)

First published by Ravette Publishing 2013.

Printed in the UK by CPI Group (UK) Ltd, Croydon, CR0 4YY
for Ravette Publishing Limited,
PO Box 876
Horsham
West Sussex RH12 9GH

ISBN: 978-1-84161-374-1

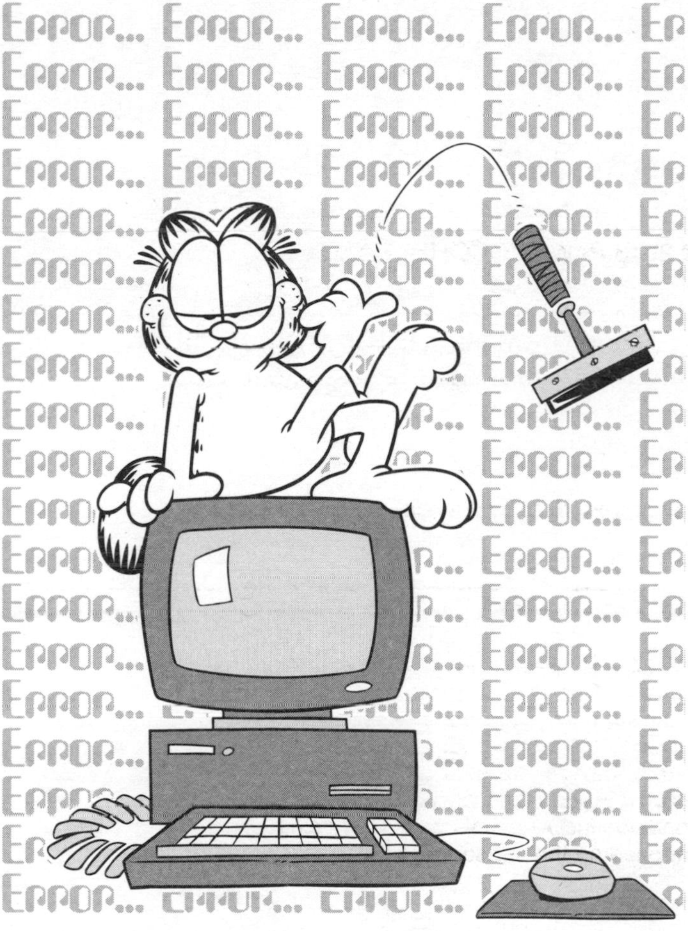
ERROR...

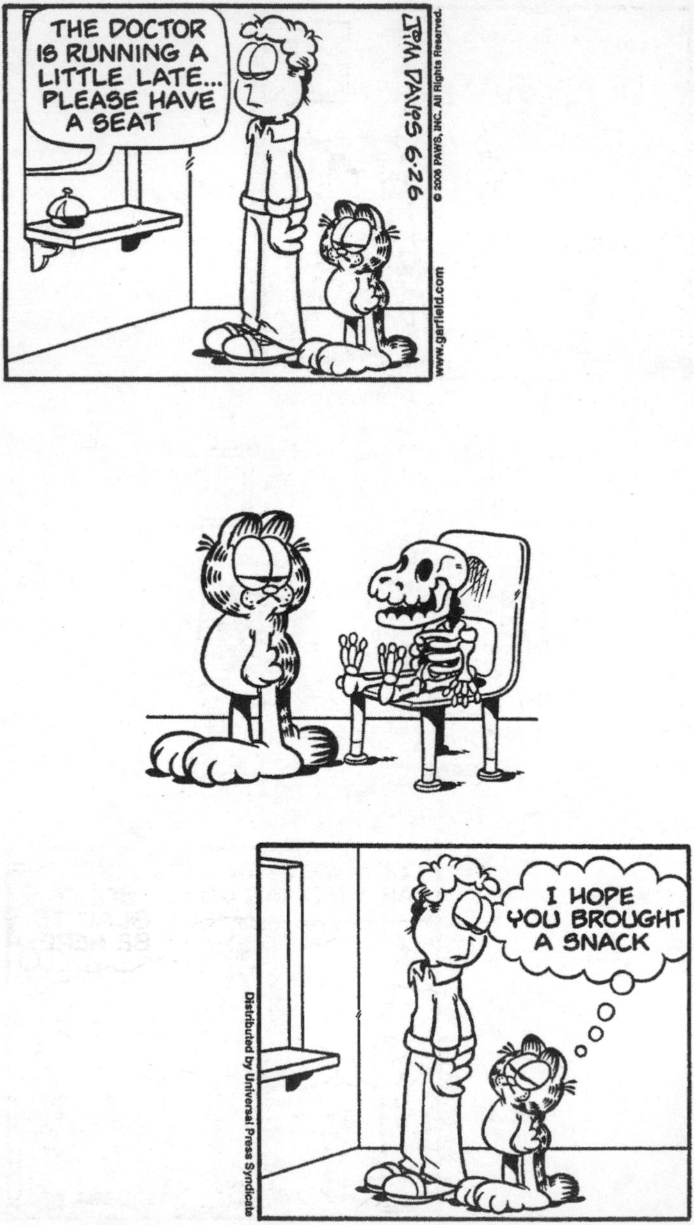
THE DOCTOR IS RUNNING A LITTLE LATE... PLEASE HAVE A SEAT
JPM DAVIS 6-26
© 2006 PAWS, INC. All Rights Reserved.
www.garfield.com
I HOPE YOU BROUGHT A SNACK
Distributed by Universal Press Syndicate

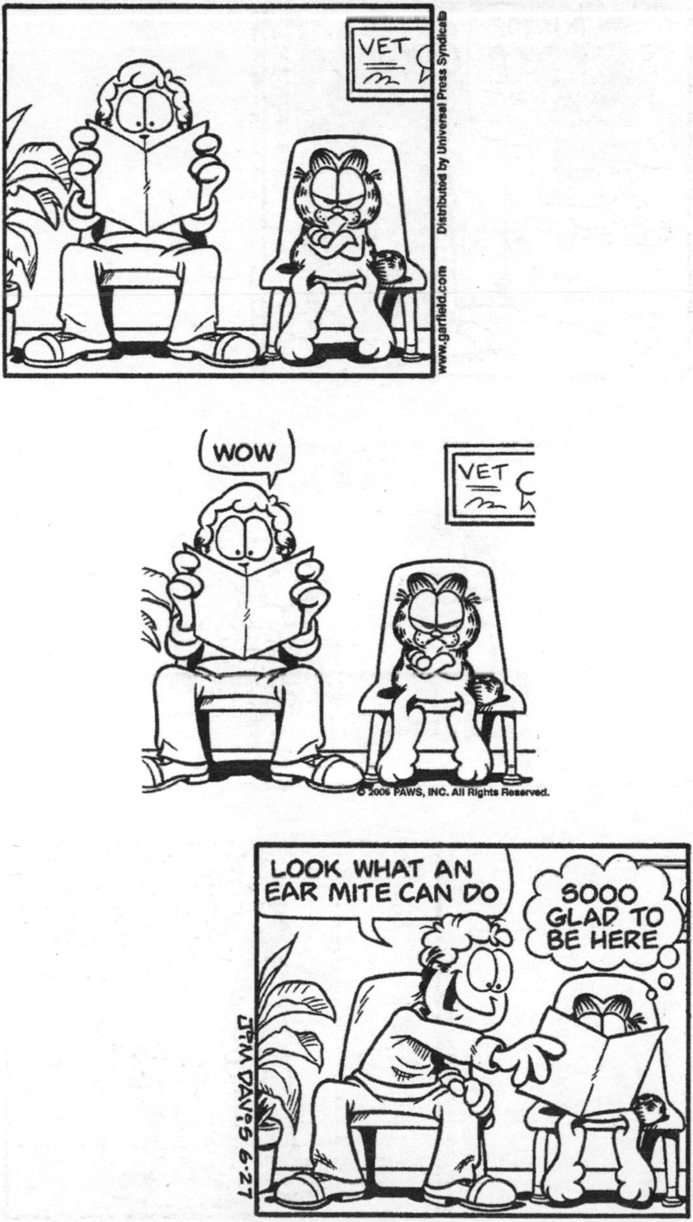
VET
Distributed by Universal Press Syndicate
www.garfield.com
WOW
VET
© 2006 PAWS, INC. All Rights Reserved.
LOOK WHAT AN EAR MITE CAN DO
SOOO GLAD TO BE HERE
JIM DAVIS 6-27

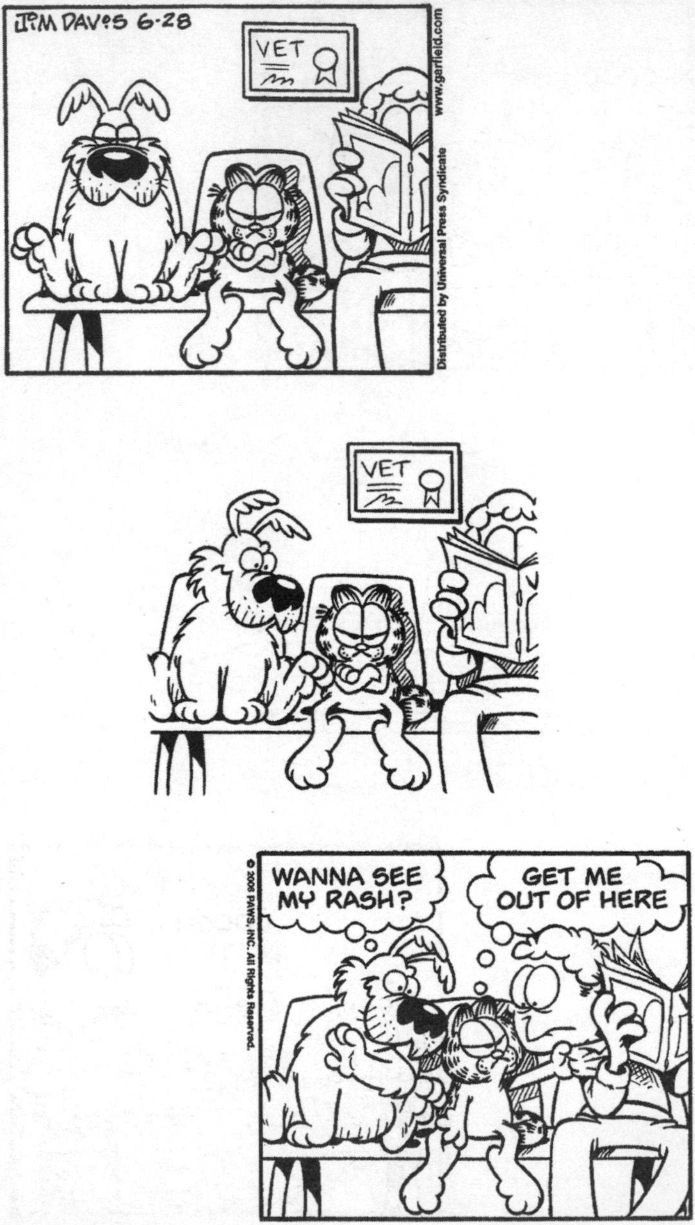
JIM DAVIS 6-28
VET
www.garfield.com
Distributed by Universal Press Syndicate
VET
© 2006 PAWS, INC. All Rights Reserved.
WANNA SEE MY RASH?
GET ME OUT OF HERE

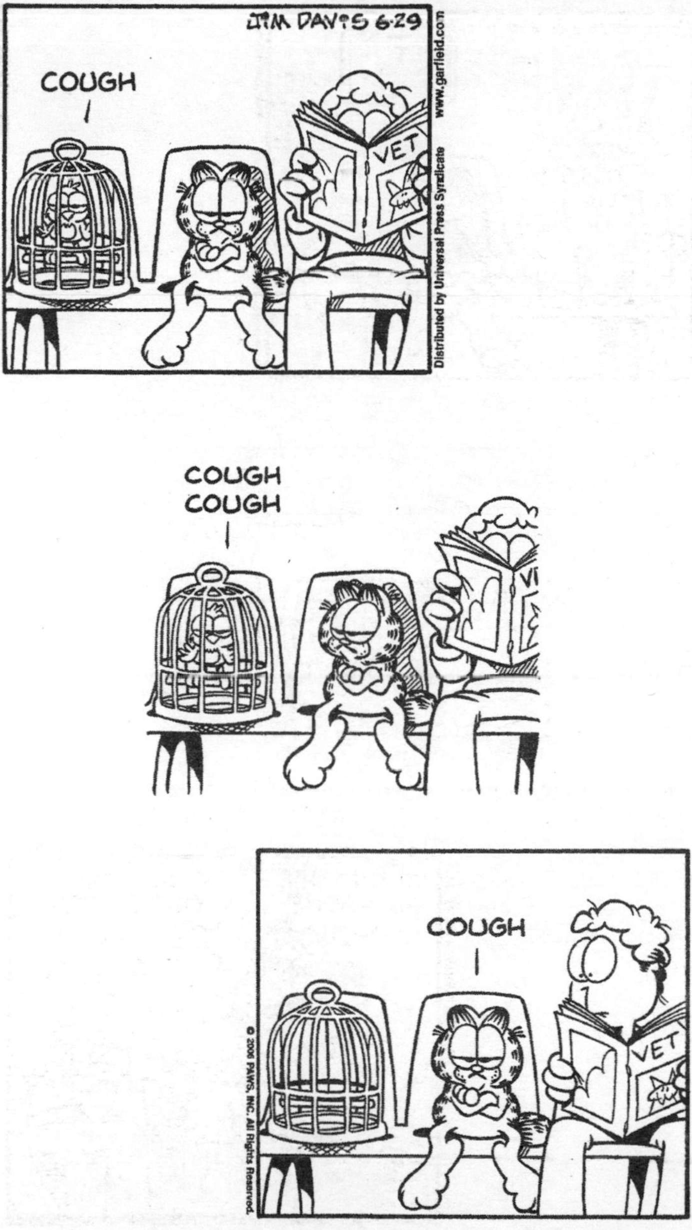
JIM DAVIS 6-29
www.garfield.com
Distributed by Universal Press Syndicate
COUGH
VET
COUGH
COUGH
COUGH
VET
© 2006 PAWS, INC. All Rights Reserved.

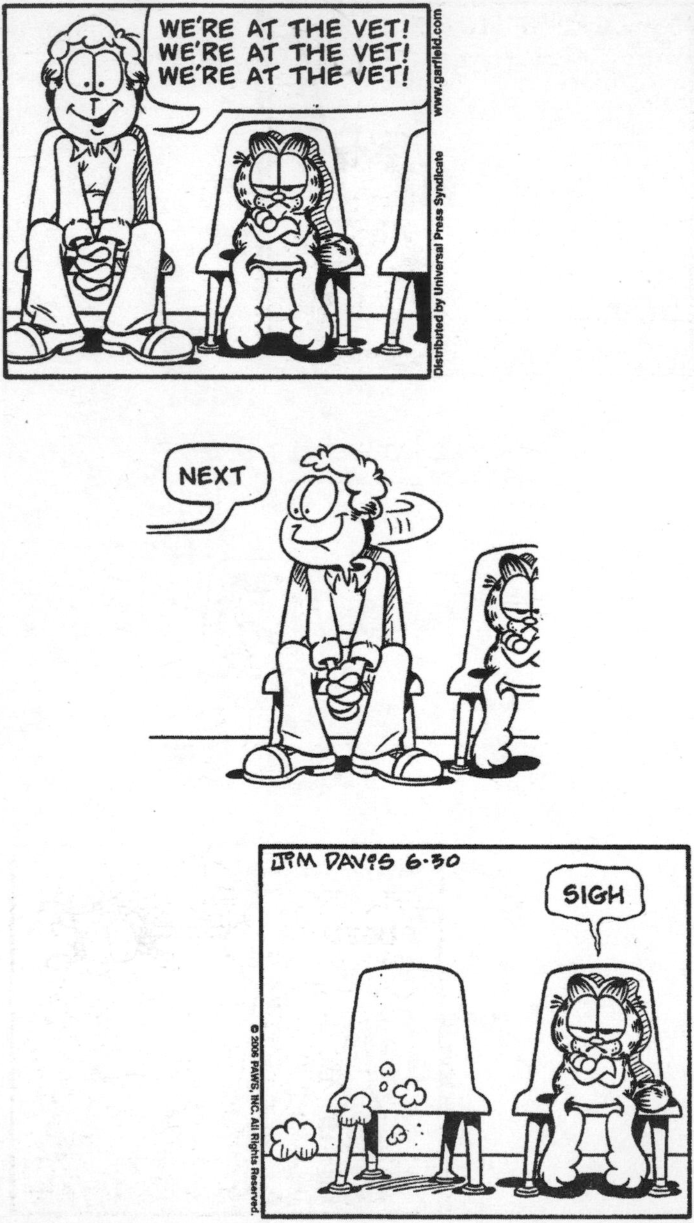
WE'RE AT THE VET! WE'RE AT THE VET! WE'RE AT THE VET!
NEXT
JIM DAVIS 6-30
SIGH

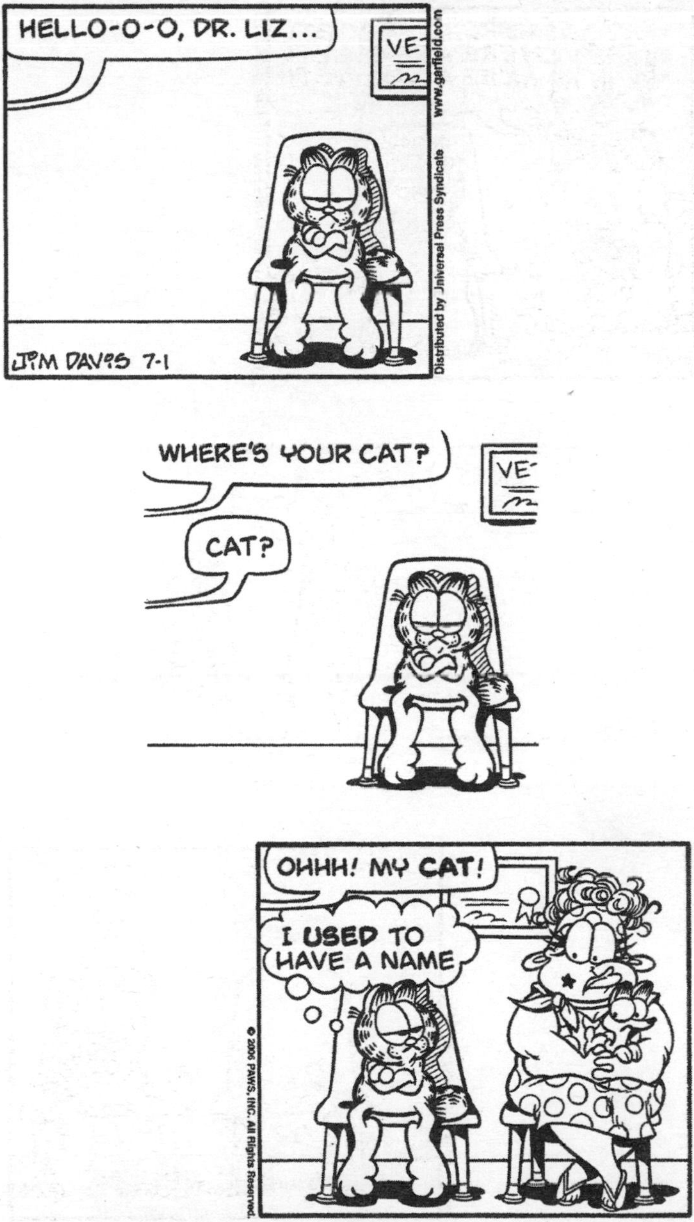
HELLO-O-O, DR. LIZ...
VET
JIM DAVIS 7-1
Distributed by Universal Press Syndicate
www.garfield.com
WHERE'S YOUR CAT?
CAT?
VET
OHHH! MY CAT!
I USED TO HAVE A NAME
© 2006 PAWS, INC. All Rights Reserved.

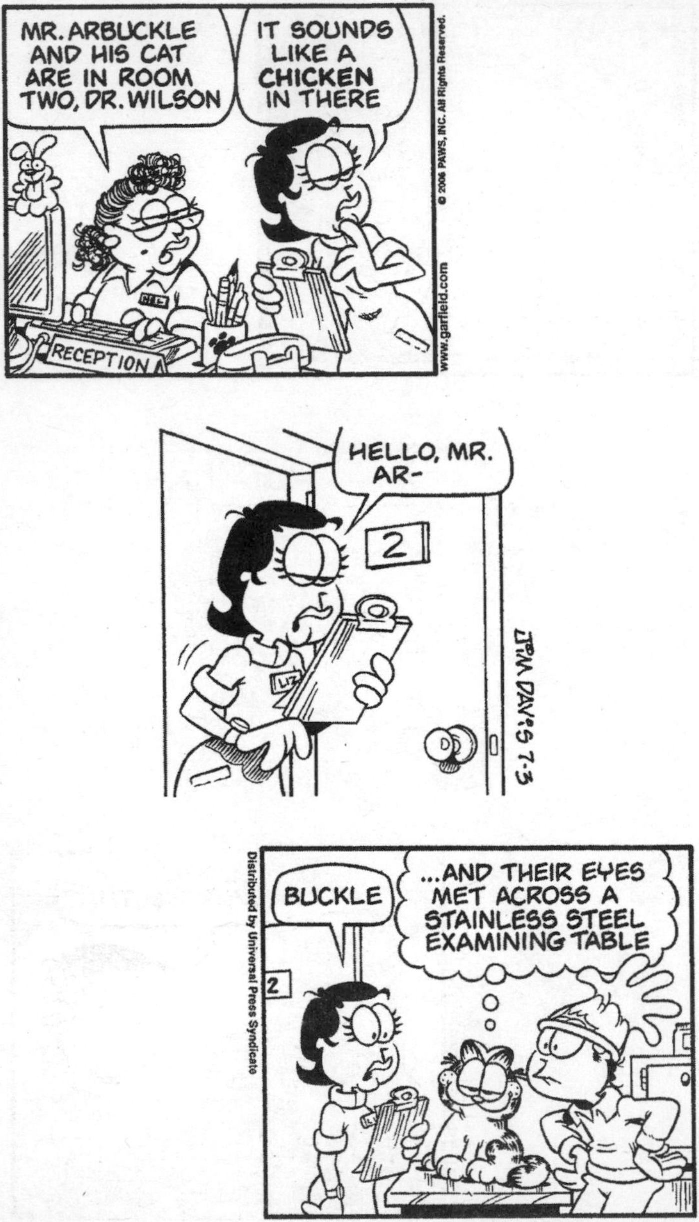
MR. ARBUCKLE AND HIS CAT ARE IN ROOM TWO, DR. WILSON
IT SOUNDS LIKE A CHICKEN IN THERE
RECEPTION
© 2006 PAWS, INC. All Rights Reserved.
www.garfield.com
HELLO, MR. AR-
2
LIZ
JPM DAVIS 7-3
Distributed by Universal Press Syndicate
BUCKLE
...AND THEIR EYES MET ACROSS A STAINLESS STEEL EXAMINING TABLE
2

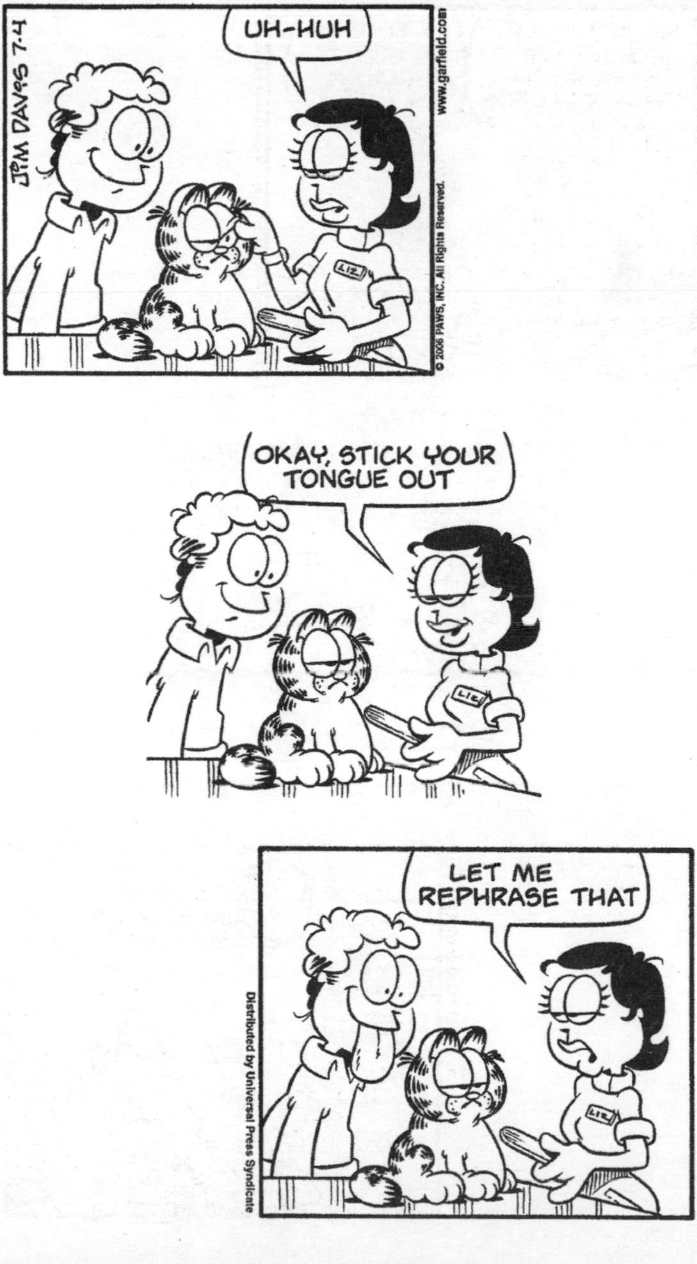
JIM DAVIS 7-4
UH-HUH
LIZ
OKAY, STICK YOUR TONGUE OUT
LIZ
LET ME REPHRASE THAT
LIZ
www.garfield.com

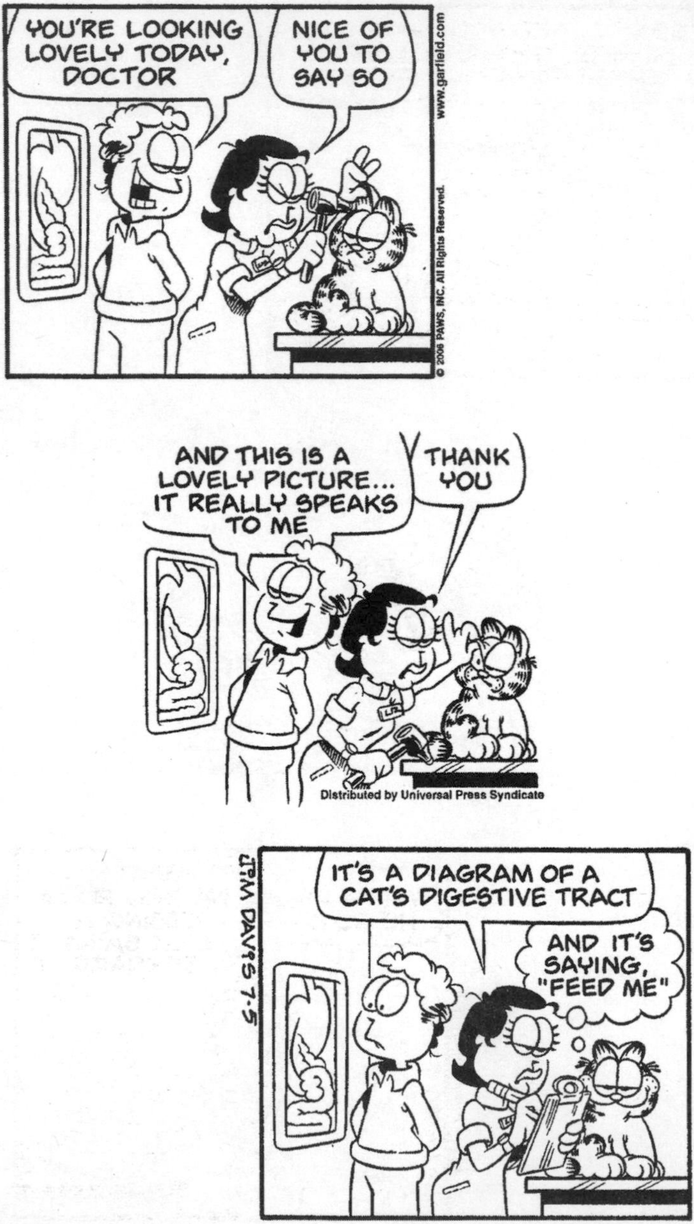
YOU'RE LOOKING LOVELY TODAY, DOCTOR
NICE OF YOU TO SAY SO
© 2006 PAWS, INC. All Rights Reserved. www.garfield.com
AND THIS IS A LOVELY PICTURE... IT REALLY SPEAKS TO ME
THANK YOU
Distributed by Universal Press Syndicate
JPM DAVIS 7-5
IT'S A DIAGRAM OF A CAT'S DIGESTIVE TRACT
AND IT'S SAYING, "FEED ME"

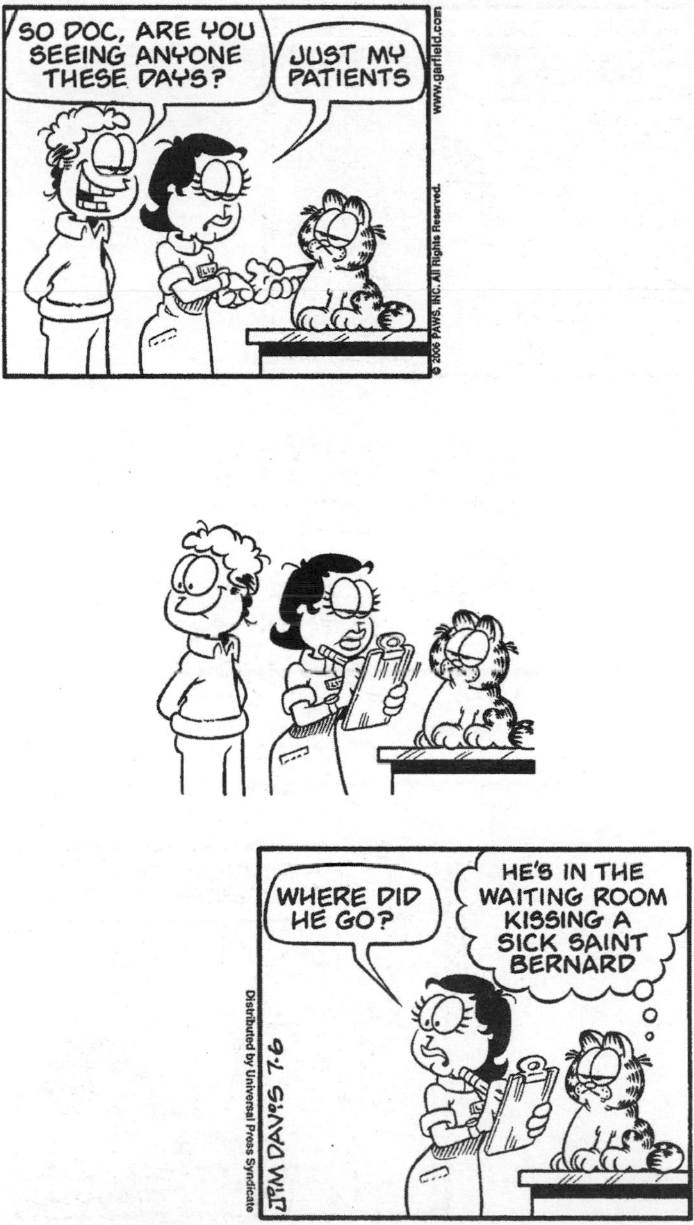
SO DOC, ARE YOU SEEING ANYONE THESE DAYS?
JUST MY PATIENTS
© 2006 PAWS, INC. All Rights Reserved. www.garfield.com
WHERE DID HE GO?
HE'S IN THE WAITING ROOM KISSING A SICK SAINT BERNARD
JIM DAVIS 7-6
Distributed by Universal Press Syndicate

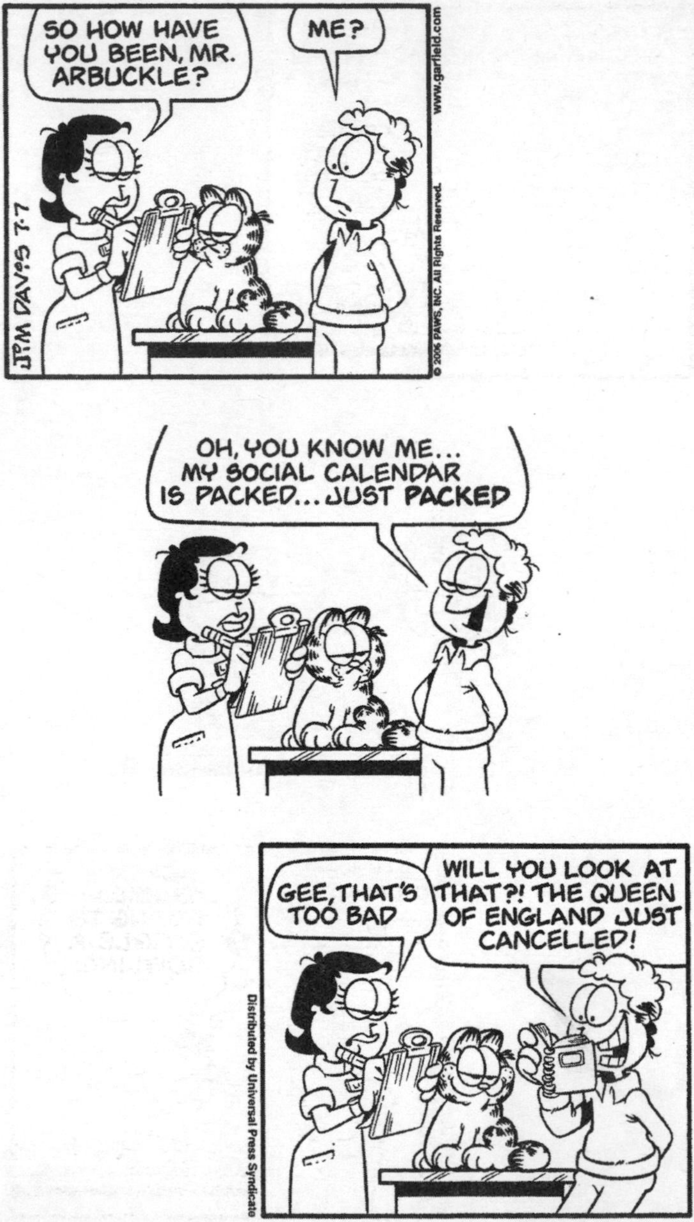
SO HOW HAVE YOU BEEN, MR. ARBUCKLE?
ME?
JIM DAVIS 7-7
© 2006 PAWS, INC. All Rights Reserved.
www.garfield.com
OH, YOU KNOW ME... MY SOCIAL CALENDAR IS PACKED... JUST PACKED
GEE, THAT'S TOO BAD
WILL YOU LOOK AT THAT?! THE QUEEN OF ENGLAND JUST CANCELLED!
Distributed by Universal Press Syndicate

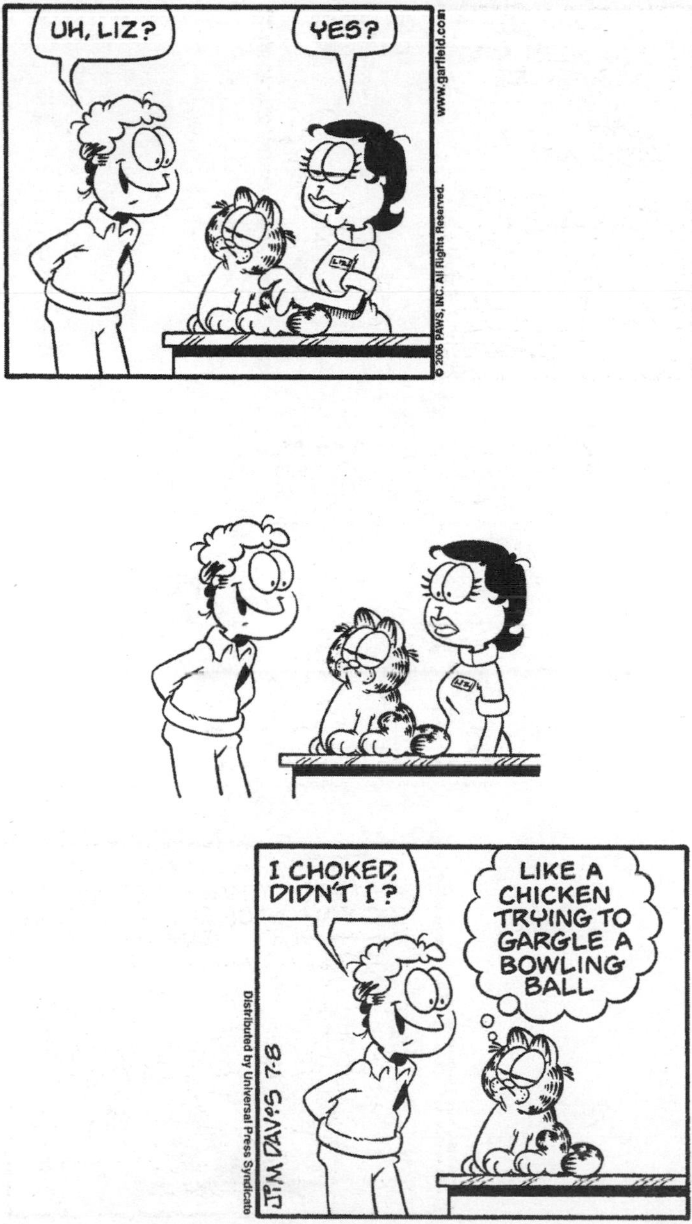

UH, LIZ?
YES?
© 2006 PAWS, INC. All Rights Reserved. www.garfield.com
I CHOKED, DIDN'T I?
LIKE A CHICKEN TRYING TO GARGLE A BOWLING BALL
JIM DAVIS 7-8
Distributed by Universal Press Syndicate

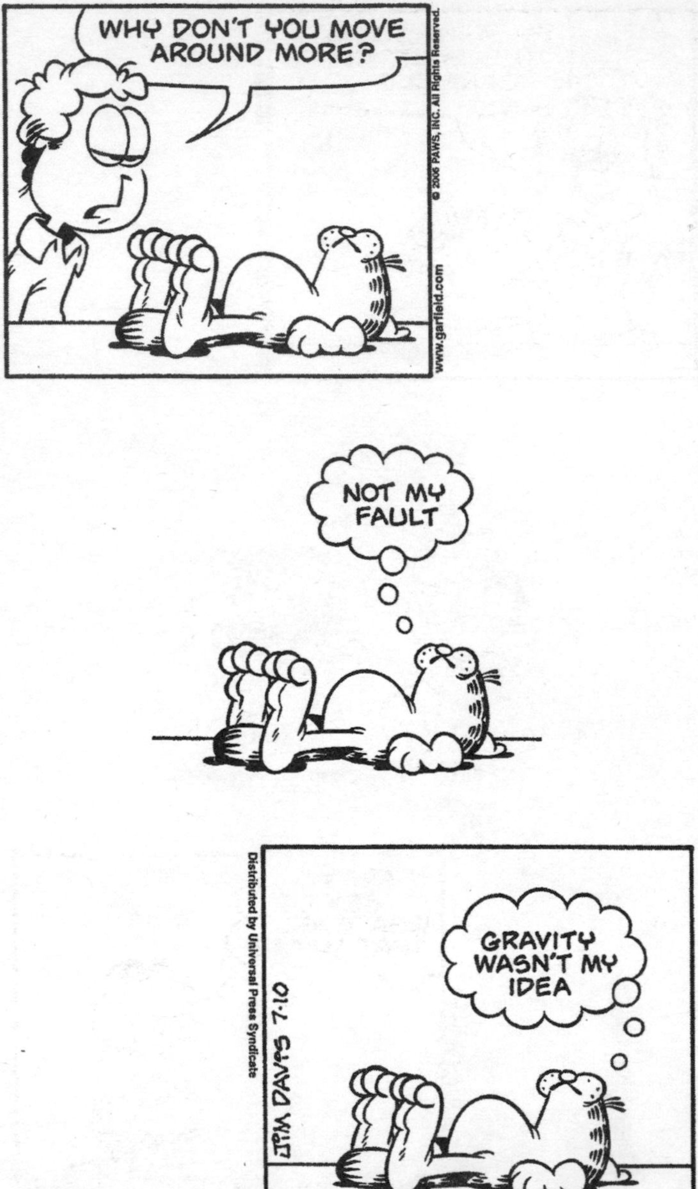
WHY DON'T YOU MOVE AROUND MORE?
© 2006 PAWS, INC. All Rights Reserved.
www.garfield.com
NOT MY FAULT
GRAVITY WASN'T MY IDEA
JIM DAVIS 7-10
Distributed by Universal Press Syndicate

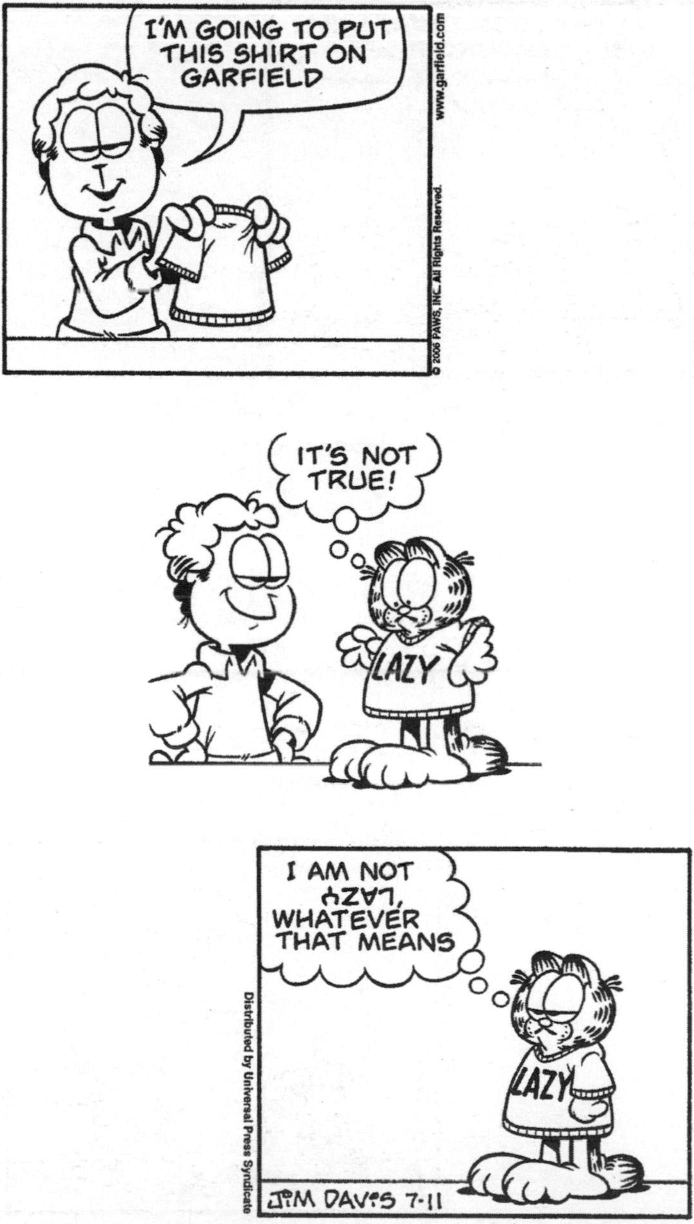

I'M GOING TO PUT THIS SHIRT ON GARFIELD
www.garfield.com
© 2006 PAWS, INC. All Rights Reserved.
IT'S NOT TRUE!
LAZY
I AM NOT ʎZ∀˥, WHATEVER THAT MEANS
LAZY
JIM DAVIS 7-11
Distributed by Universal Press Syndicate

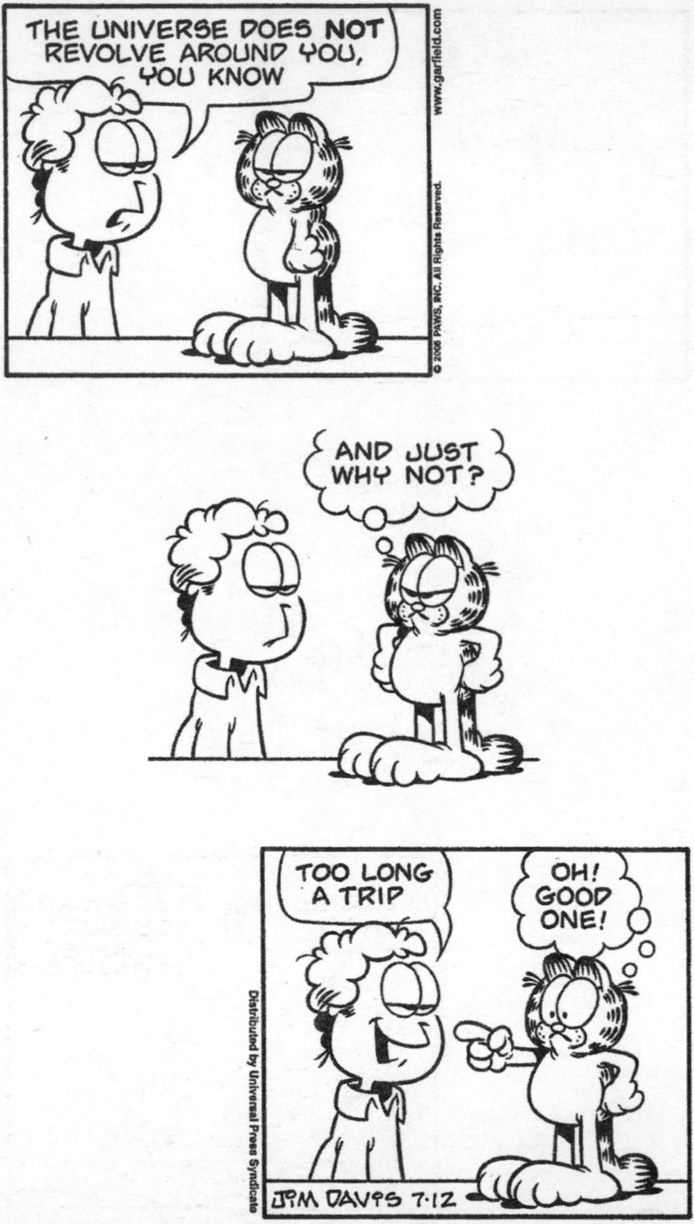
THE UNIVERSE DOES NOT REVOLVE AROUND YOU, YOU KNOW
www.garfield.com
© 2006 PAWS, INC. All Rights Reserved.
AND JUST WHY NOT?
TOO LONG A TRIP
OH! GOOD ONE!
JIM DAVIS 7·12
Distributed by Universal Press Syndicate

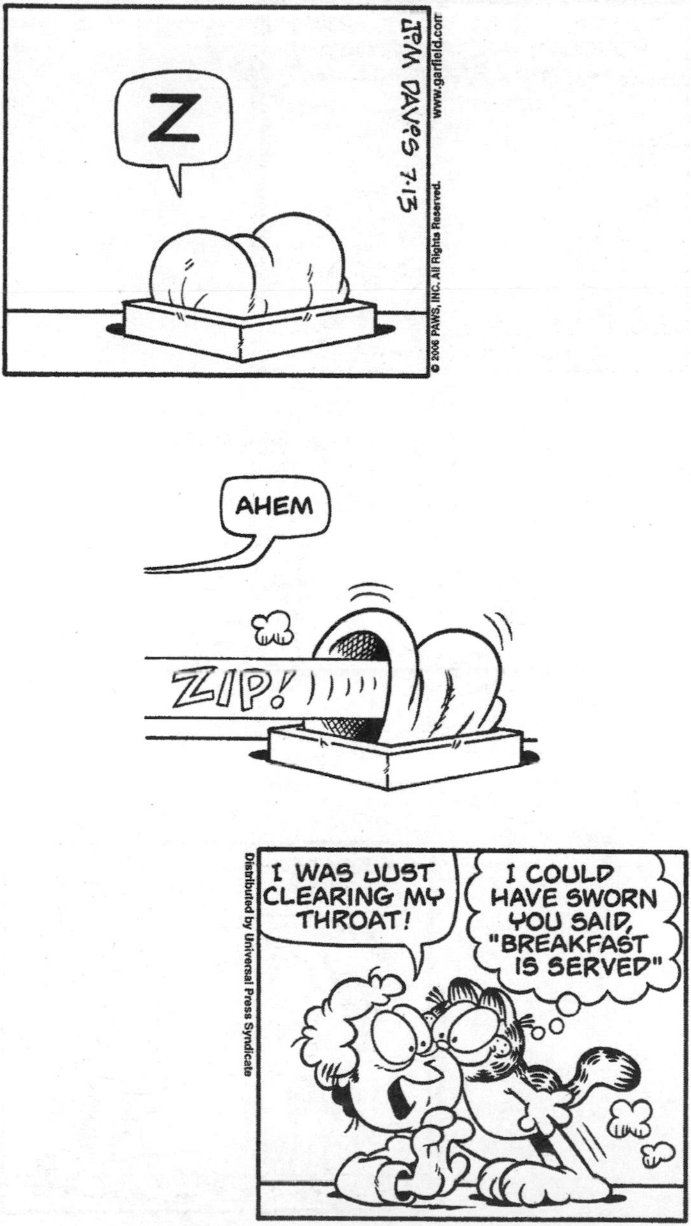
Z
JPM DAVIS 7-13
www.garfield.com
© 2006 PAWS, INC. All Rights Reserved.
AHEM
ZIP!
Distributed by Universal Press Syndicate
I WAS JUST CLEARING MY THROAT!
I COULD HAVE SWORN YOU SAID, "BREAKFAST IS SERVED"

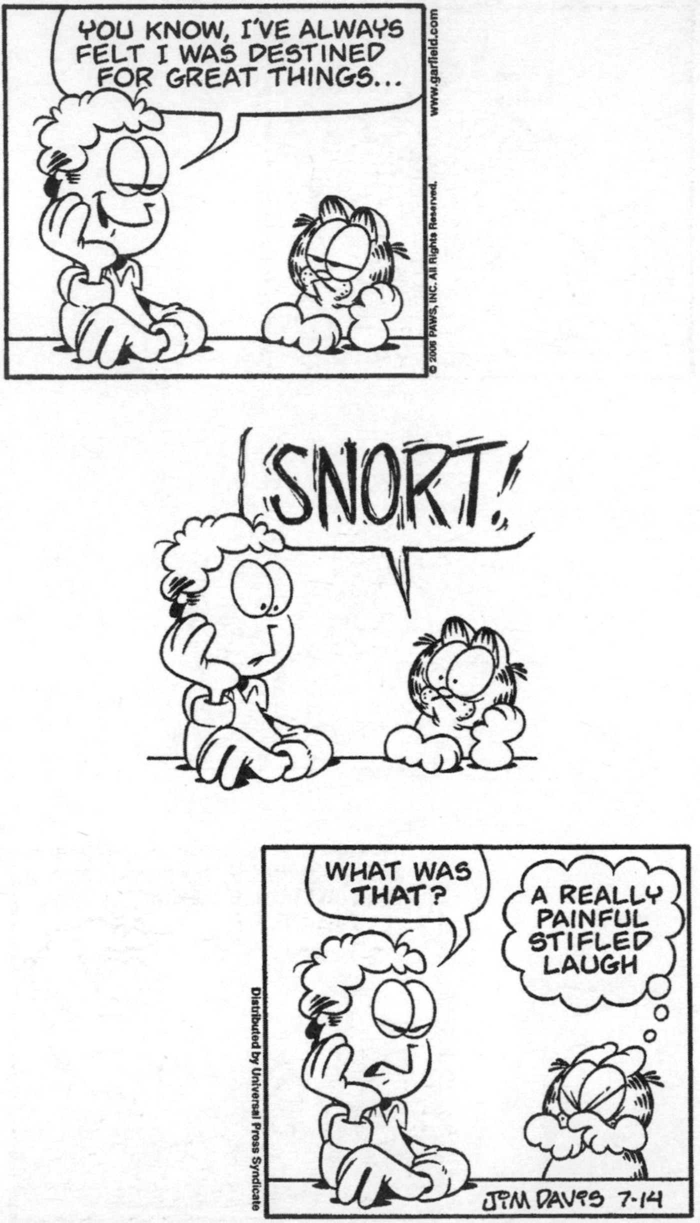
YOU KNOW, I'VE ALWAYS FELT I WAS DESTINED FOR GREAT THINGS...
© 2006 PAWS, INC. All Rights Reserved. www.garfield.com
SNORT!
WHAT WAS THAT?
A REALLY PAINFUL STIFLED LAUGH
Distributed by Universal Press Syndicate
JIM DAVIS 7-14

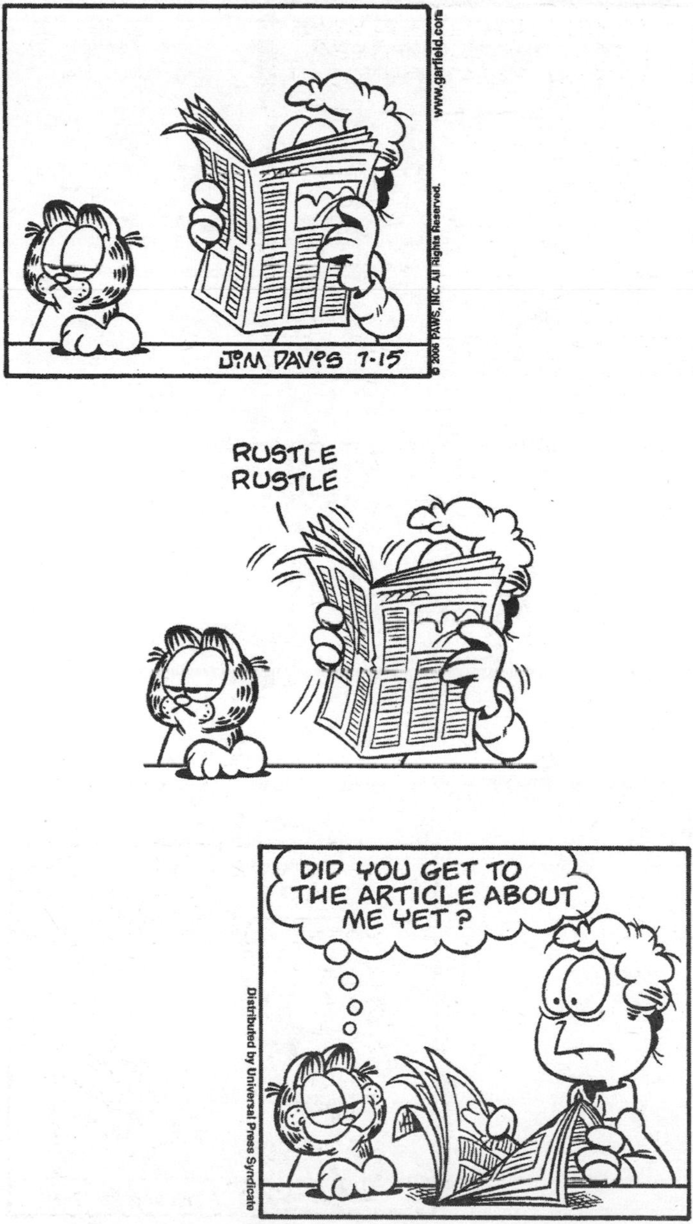
JIM DAVIS 7-15
© 2006 PAWS, INC. All Rights Reserved.
www.garfield.com
RUSTLE RUSTLE
DID YOU GET TO THE ARTICLE ABOUT ME YET?
Distributed by Universal Press Syndicate

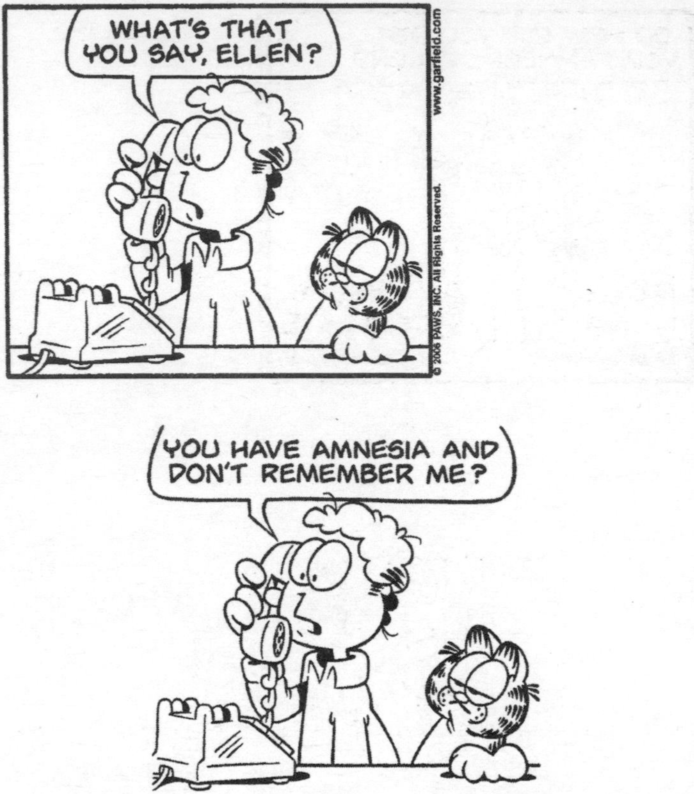
WHAT'S THAT YOU SAY, ELLEN?
© 2006 PAWS, INC. All Rights Reserved.
www.garfield.com
YOU HAVE AMNESIA AND DON'T REMEMBER ME?
COOL!
TALK ABOUT A DARK CLOUD HAVING A SILVER LINING!
JIM DAVIS 7-17
Distributed by Universal Press Syndicate

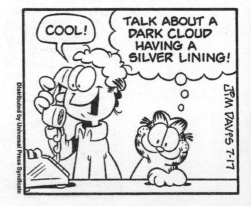

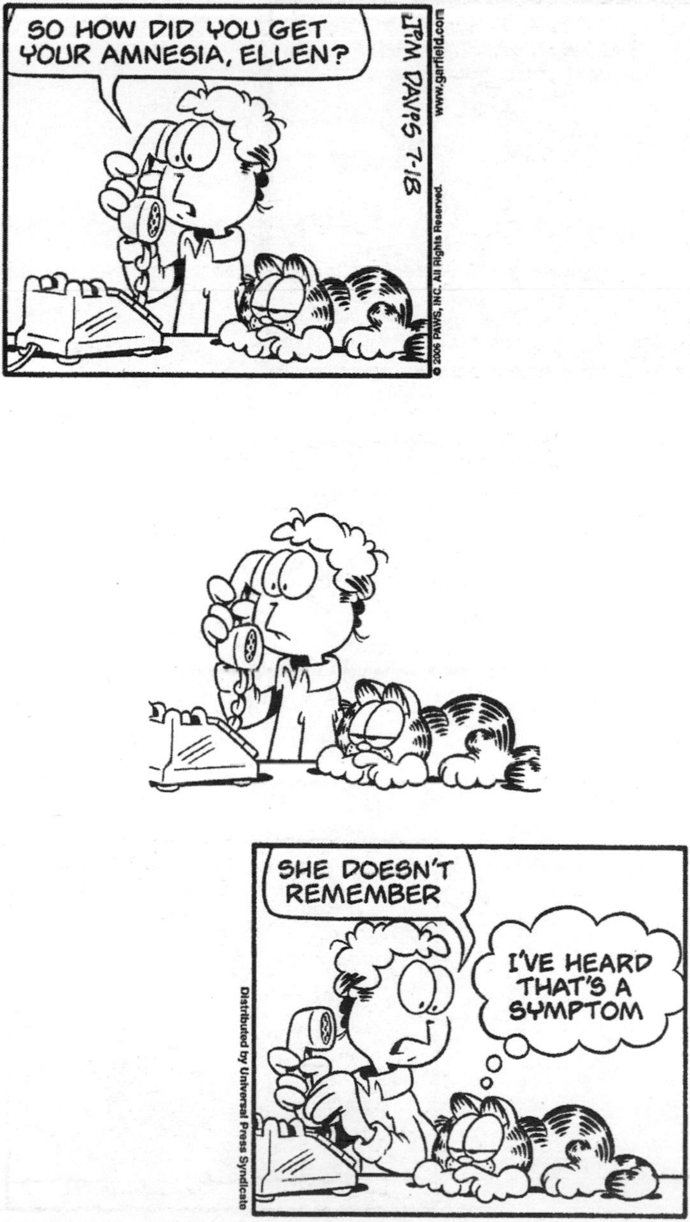
SO HOW DID YOU GET YOUR AMNESIA, ELLEN?
JIM DAVIS 7-18
www.garfield.com
© 2006 PAWS, INC. All Rights Reserved.
SHE DOESN'T REMEMBER
I'VE HEARD THAT'S A SYMPTOM
Distributed by Universal Press Syndicate

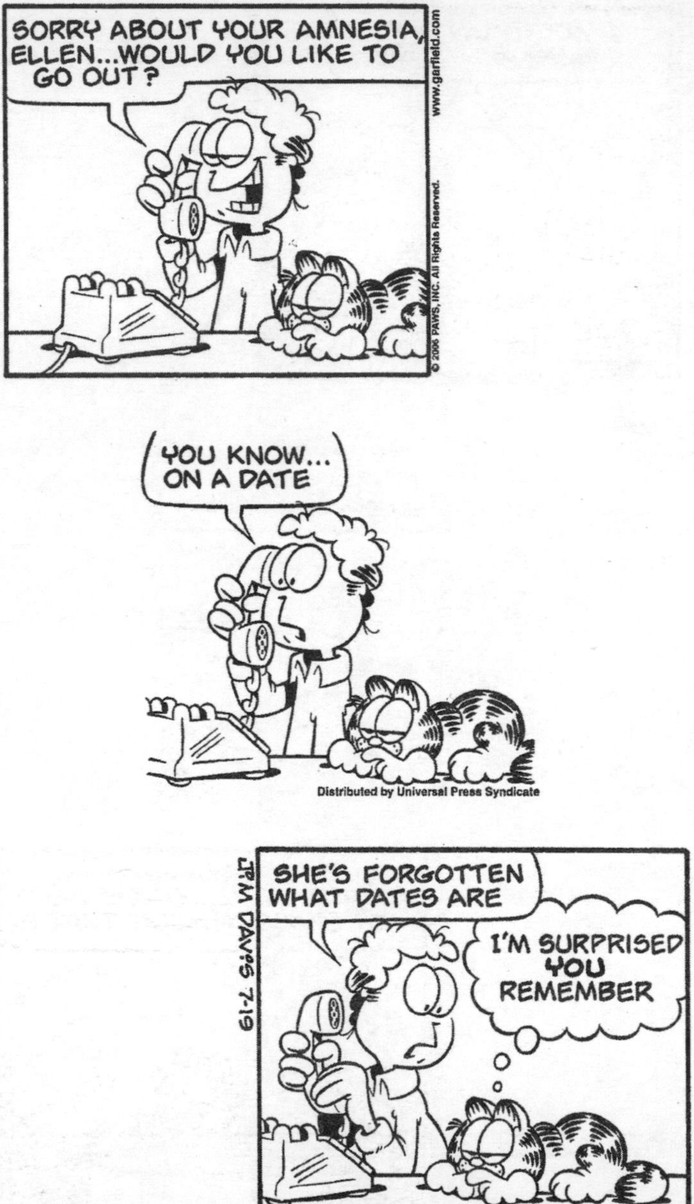
SORRY ABOUT YOUR AMNESIA, ELLEN...WOULD YOU LIKE TO GO OUT?
www.garfield.com
© 2006 PAWS, INC. All Rights Reserved.
YOU KNOW... ON A DATE
Distributed by Universal Press Syndicate
JIM DAVIS 7-19
SHE'S FORGOTTEN WHAT DATES ARE
I'M SURPRISED YOU REMEMBER

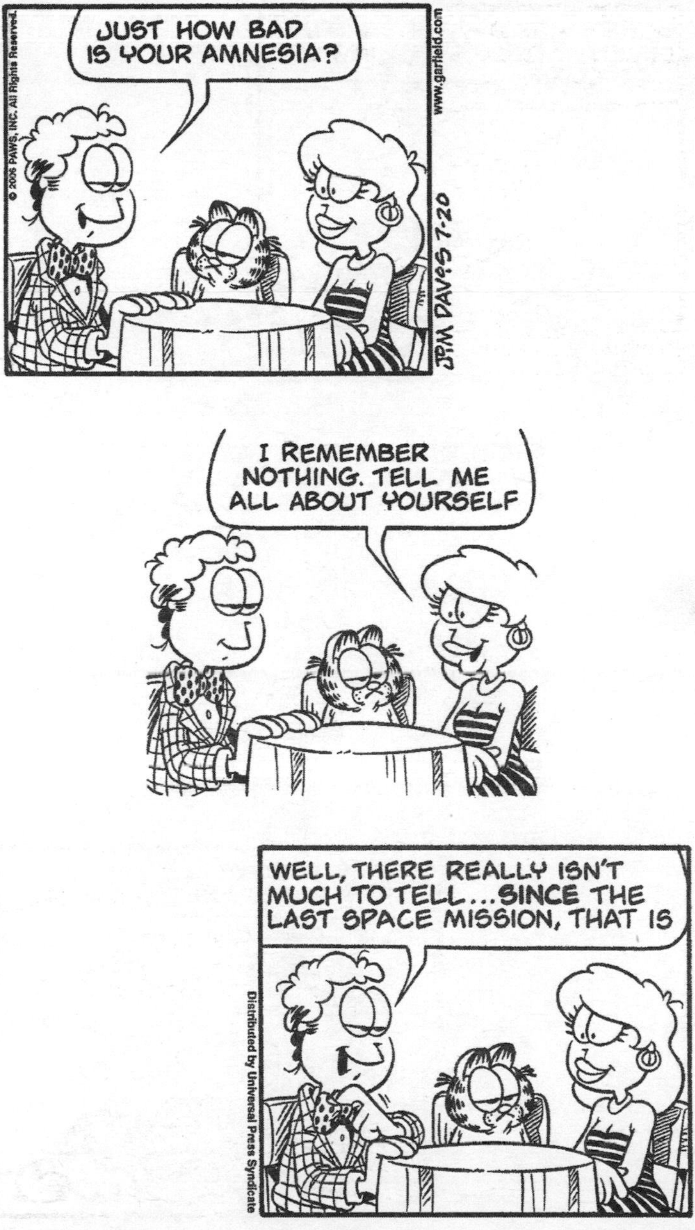
© 2006 PAWS, INC. All Rights Reserved.
JUST HOW BAD IS YOUR AMNESIA?
www.garfield.com
JIM DAVIS 7-20
I REMEMBER NOTHING. TELL ME ALL ABOUT YOURSELF
WELL, THERE REALLY ISN'T MUCH TO TELL...SINCE THE LAST SPACE MISSION, THAT IS
Distributed by Universal Press Syndicate

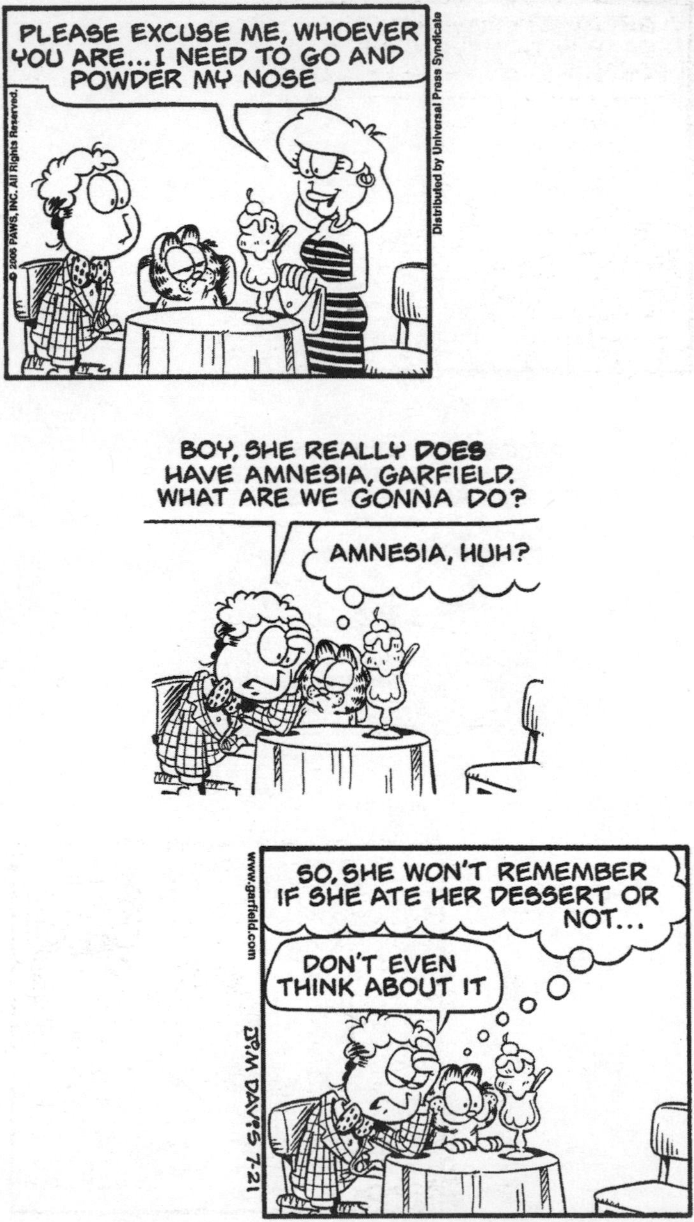
PLEASE EXCUSE ME, WHOEVER YOU ARE... I NEED TO GO AND POWDER MY NOSE
© 2006 PAWS, INC. All Rights Reserved.
Distributed by Universal Press Syndicate
BOY, SHE REALLY DOES HAVE AMNESIA, GARFIELD. WHAT ARE WE GONNA DO?
AMNESIA, HUH?
www.garfield.com
SO, SHE WON'T REMEMBER IF SHE ATE HER DESSERT OR NOT...
DON'T EVEN THINK ABOUT IT
JIM DAVIS 7-21

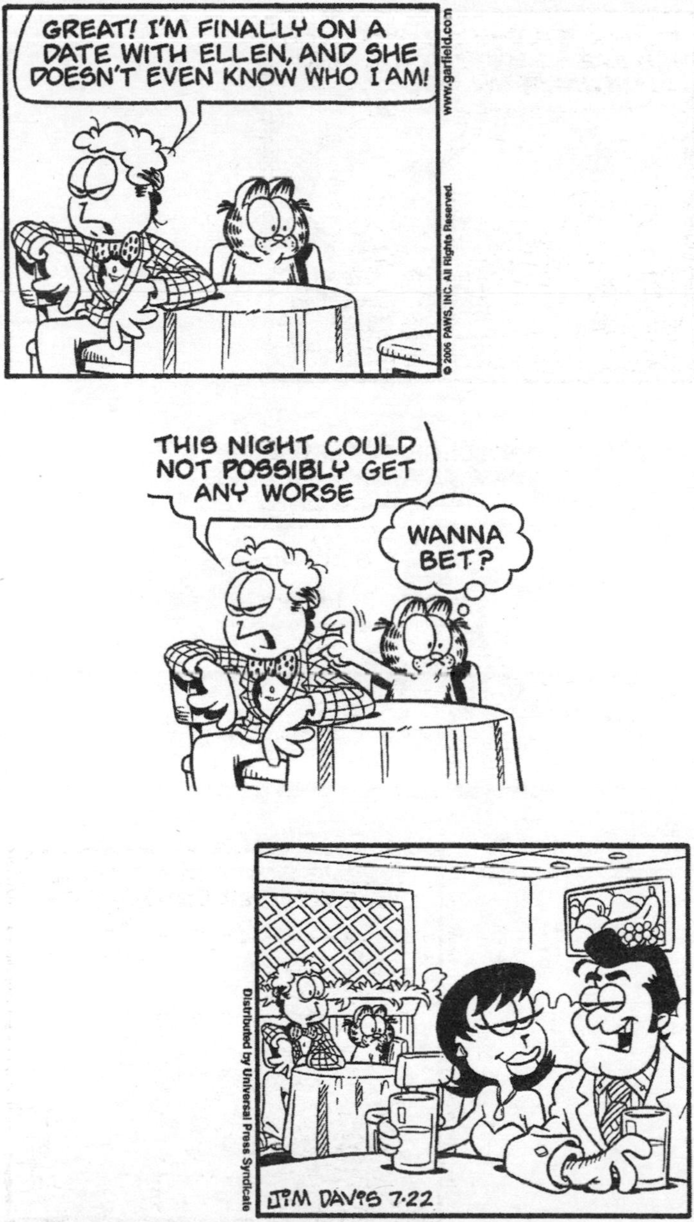
GREAT! I'M FINALLY ON A DATE WITH ELLEN, AND SHE DOESN'T EVEN KNOW WHO I AM!
© 2006 PAWS, INC. All Rights Reserved. www.garfield.com
THIS NIGHT COULD NOT POSSIBLY GET ANY WORSE
WANNA BET?
Distributed by Universal Press Syndicate
JIM DAVIS 7·22

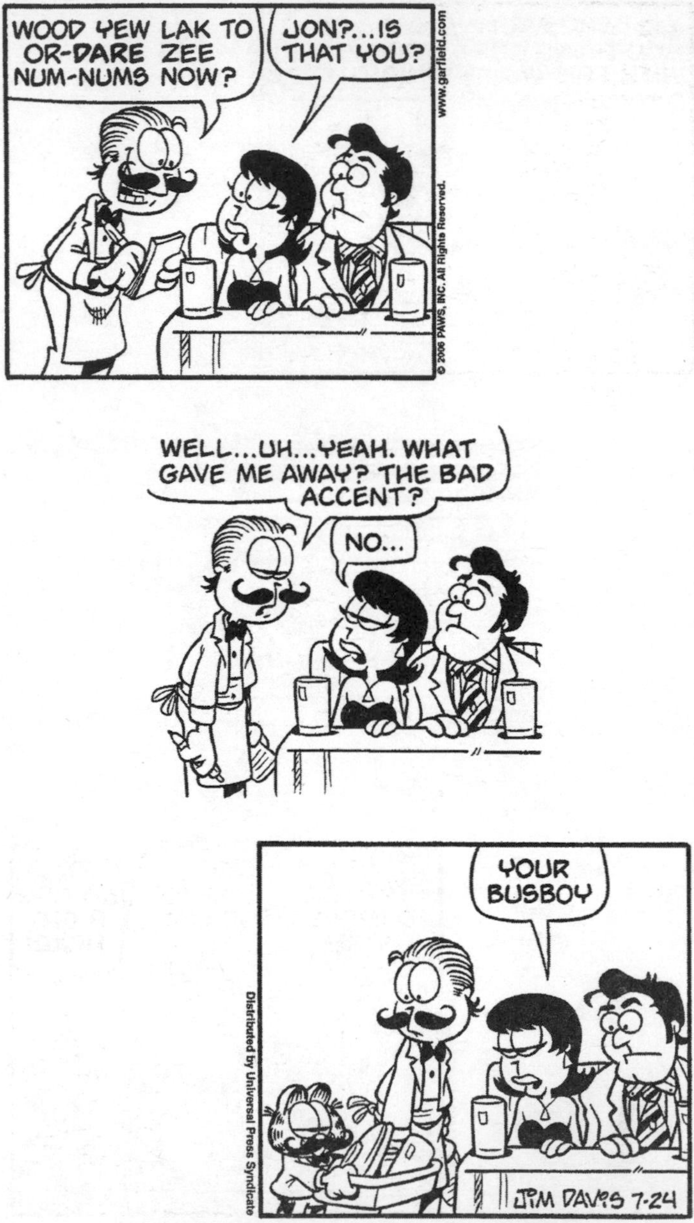
WOOD YEW LAK TO OR-DARE ZEE NUM-NUMS NOW?
JON?...IS THAT YOU?
www.garfield.com
© 2006 PAWS, INC. All Rights Reserved.
WELL...UH...YEAH. WHAT GAVE ME AWAY? THE BAD ACCENT?
NO...
YOUR BUSBOY
Distributed by Universal Press Syndicate
JIM DAVIS 7-24

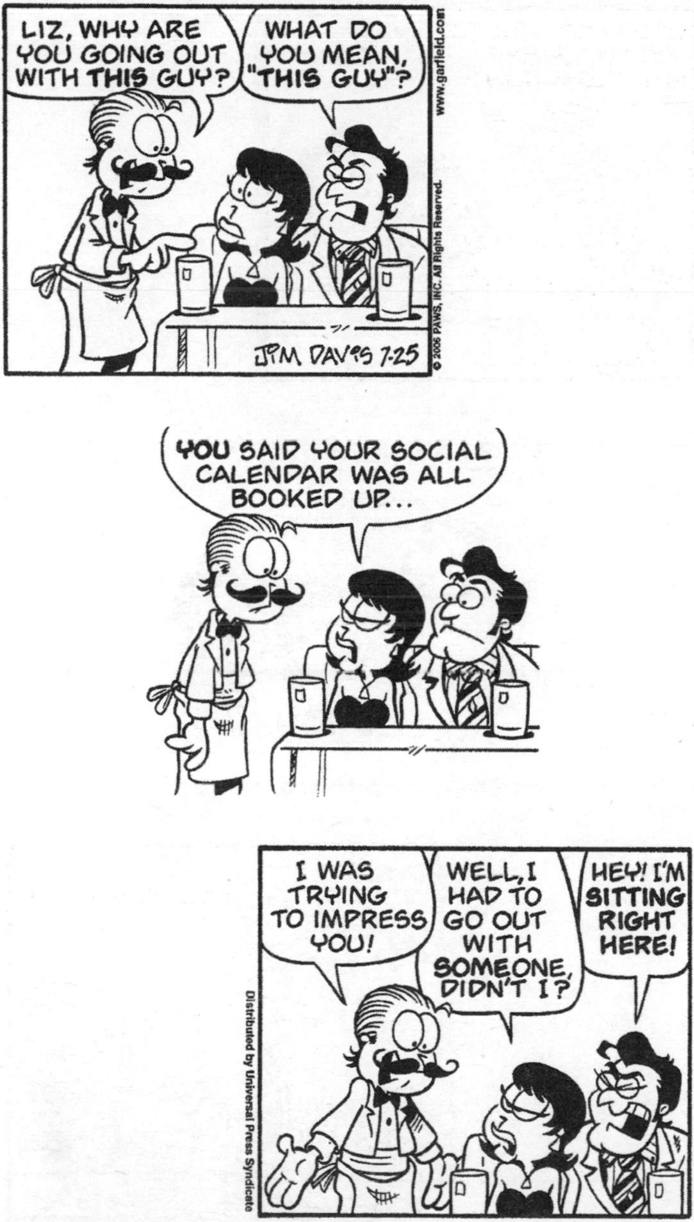
LIZ, WHY ARE YOU GOING OUT WITH THIS GUY?
WHAT DO YOU MEAN, "THIS GUY"?
JIM DAVIS 7-25
© 2006 PAWS, INC. All Rights Reserved. www.garfield.com
YOU SAID YOUR SOCIAL CALENDAR WAS ALL BOOKED UP...
I WAS TRYING TO IMPRESS YOU!
WELL, I HAD TO GO OUT WITH SOMEONE, DIDN'T I?
HEY! I'M SITTING RIGHT HERE!
Distributed by Universal Press Syndicate

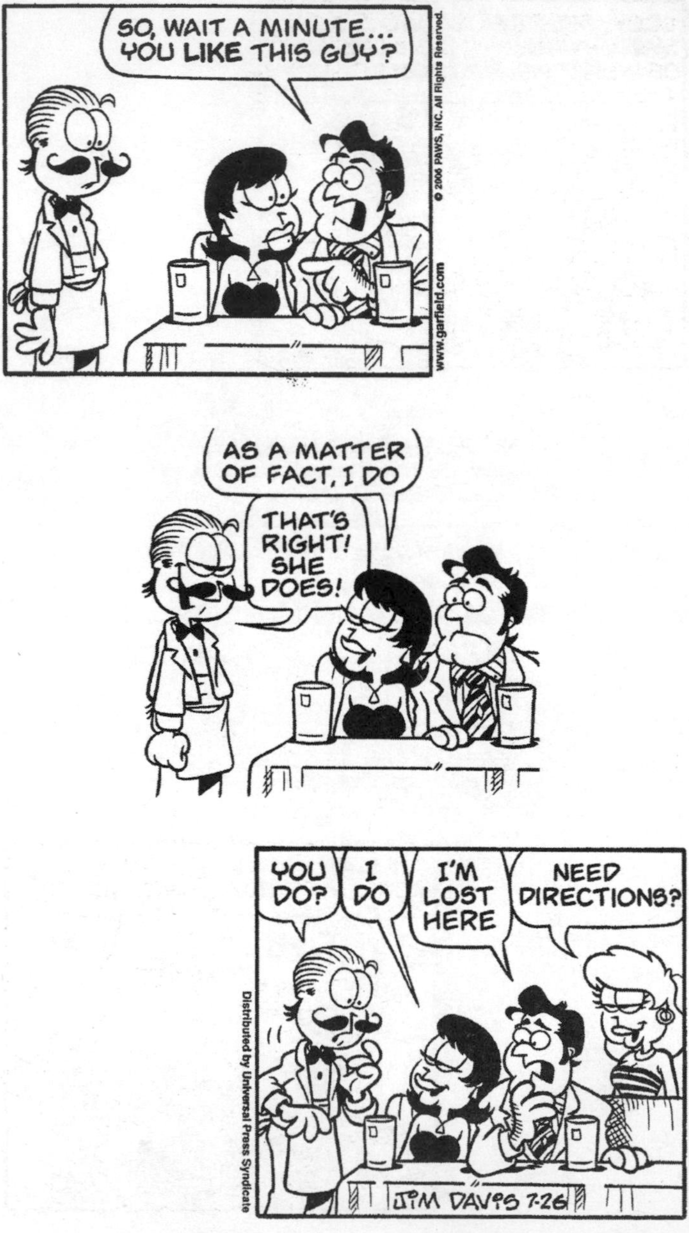
SO, WAIT A MINUTE... YOU LIKE THIS GUY?
© 2006 PAWS, INC. All Rights Reserved.
www.garfield.com
AS A MATTER OF FACT, I DO
THAT'S RIGHT! SHE DOES!
YOU DO?
I DO
I'M LOST HERE
NEED DIRECTIONS?
JIM DAVIS 7-26
Distributed by Universal Press Syndicate

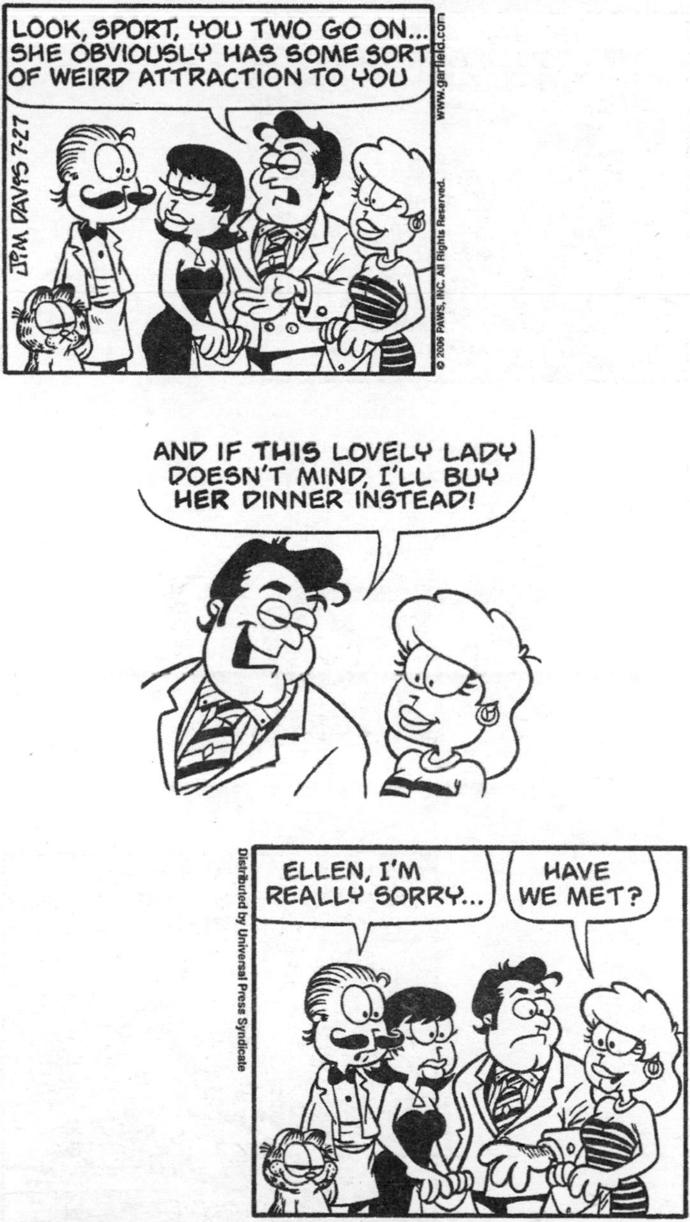
LOOK, SPORT, YOU TWO GO ON... SHE OBVIOUSLY HAS SOME SORT OF WEIRD ATTRACTION TO YOU
JIM DAVIS 7-27
© 2006 PAWS, INC. All Rights Reserved. www.garfield.com
AND IF THIS LOVELY LADY DOESN'T MIND, I'LL BUY HER DINNER INSTEAD!
ELLEN, I'M REALLY SORRY...
HAVE WE MET?
Distributed by Universal Press Syndicate

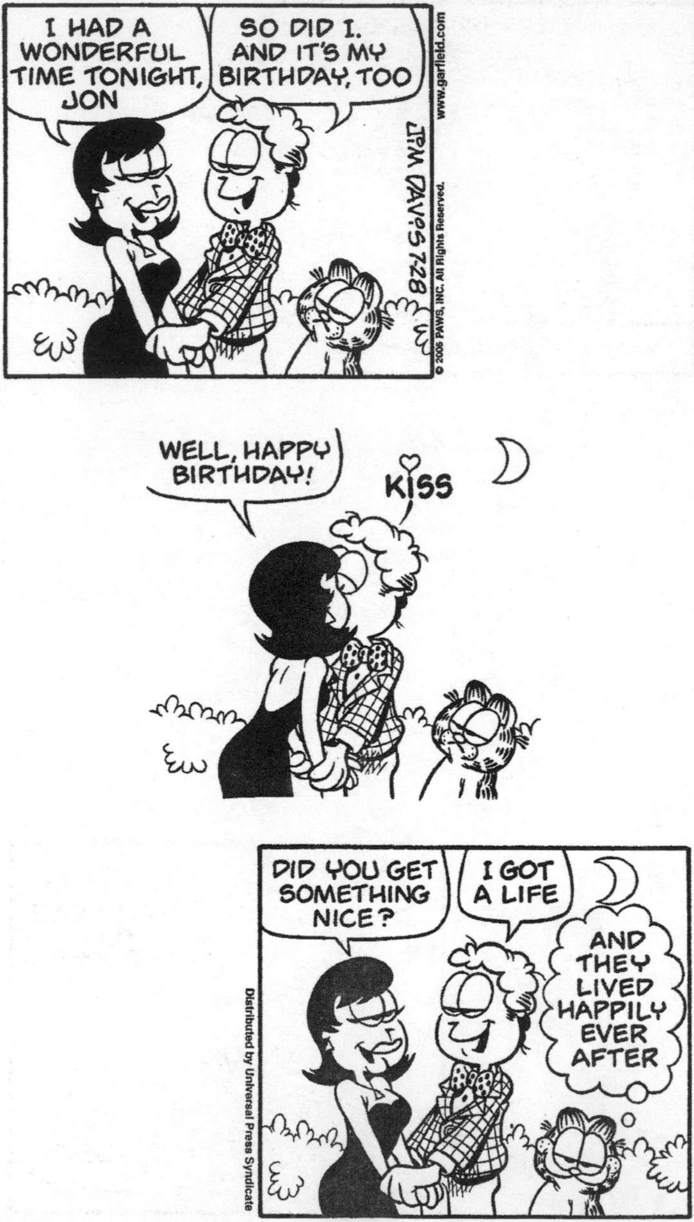
I HAD A WONDERFUL TIME TONIGHT, JON
SO DID I. AND IT'S MY BIRTHDAY, TOO
JIM DAVIS 7-28
© 2006 PAWS, INC. All Rights Reserved.
www.garfield.com
WELL, HAPPY BIRTHDAY!
KISS
DID YOU GET SOMETHING NICE?
I GOT A LIFE
AND THEY LIVED HAPPILY EVER AFTER
Distributed by Universal Press Syndicate

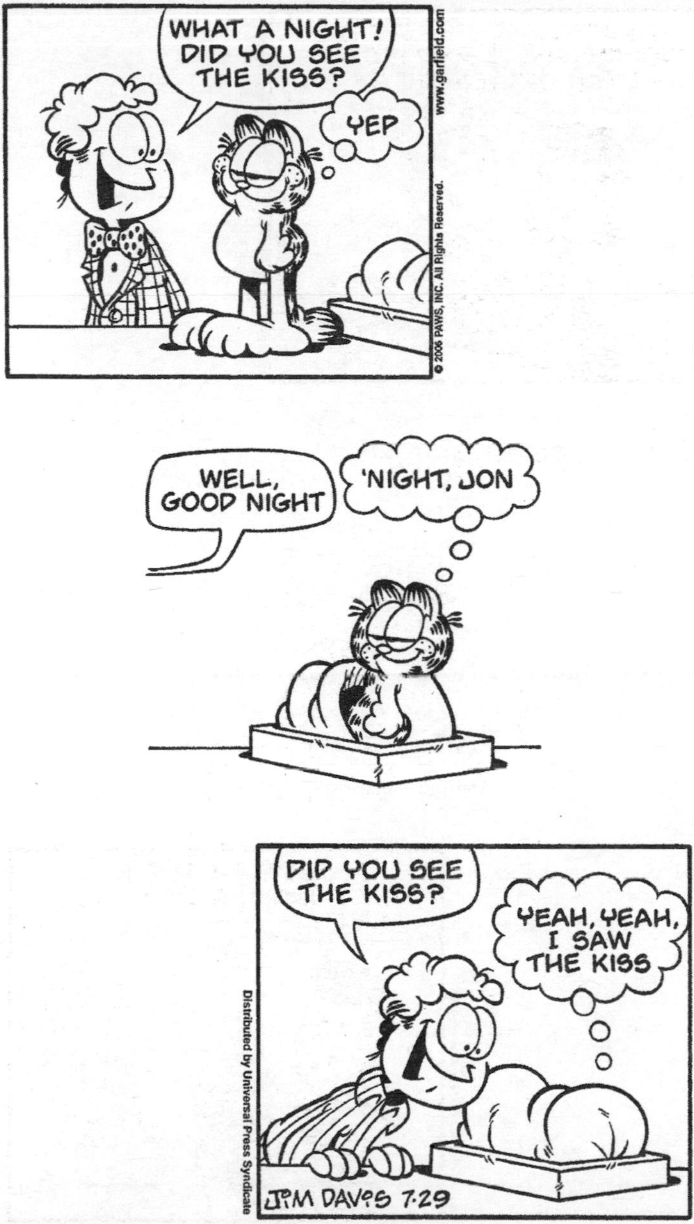

WHAT A NIGHT! DID YOU SEE THE KISS?
YEP
© 2006 PAWS, INC. All Rights Reserved.
www.garfield.com
WELL, GOOD NIGHT
'NIGHT, JON
DID YOU SEE THE KISS?
YEAH, YEAH, I SAW THE KISS
Distributed by Universal Press Syndicate
JIM DAVIS 7·29

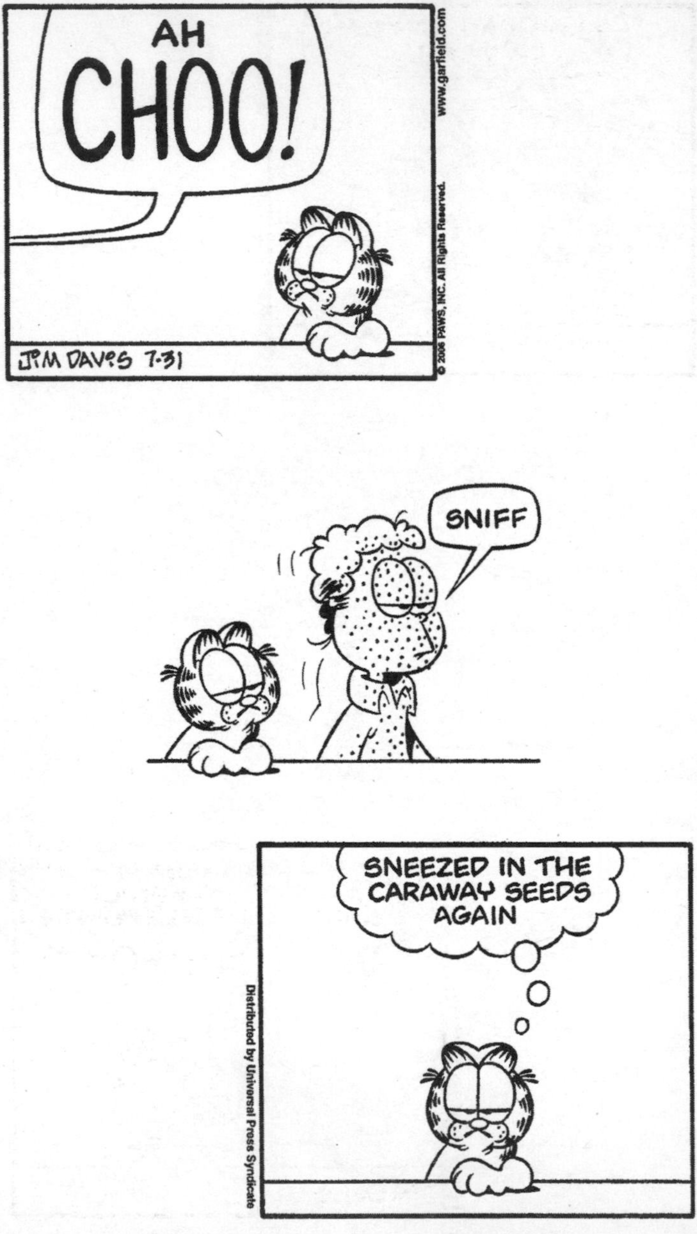
AH CHOO!
JIM DAVIS 7-31
© 2006 PAWS, INC. All Rights Reserved. www.garfield.com
SNIFF
SNEEZED IN THE CARAWAY SEEDS AGAIN
Distributed by Universal Press Syndicate

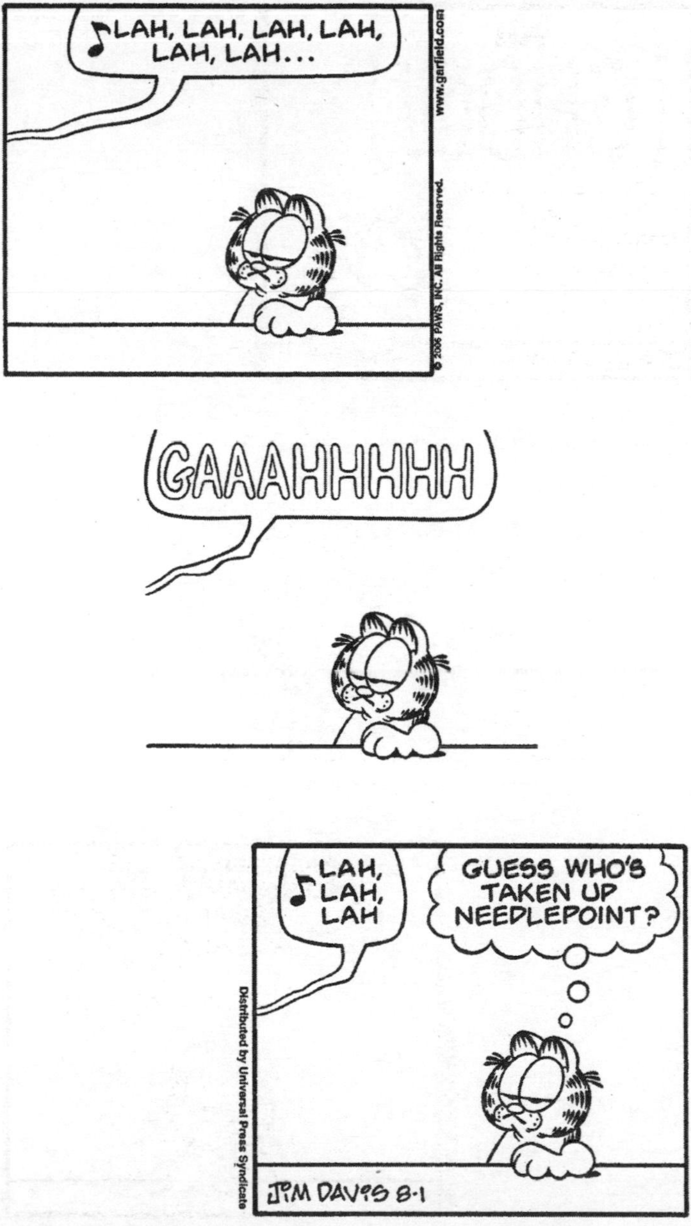
♪LAH, LAH, LAH, LAH, LAH, LAH...
GAAAHHHHH
♪LAH, LAH, LAH
GUESS WHO'S TAKEN UP NEEDLEPOINT?
JIM DAVIS 8-1

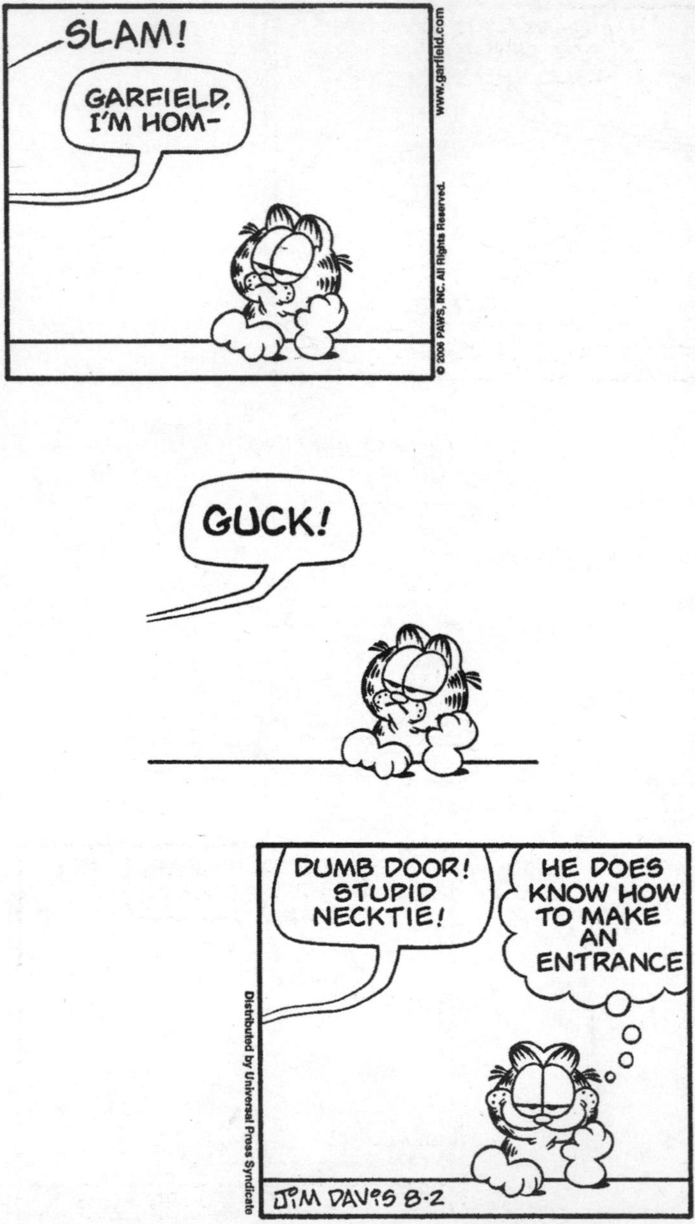
SLAM!
GARFIELD, I'M HOM-
© 2006 PAWS, INC. All Rights Reserved.
www.garfield.com
GUCK!
DUMB DOOR! STUPID NECKTIE!
HE DOES KNOW HOW TO MAKE AN ENTRANCE
JIM DAVIS 8-2
Distributed by Universal Press Syndicate

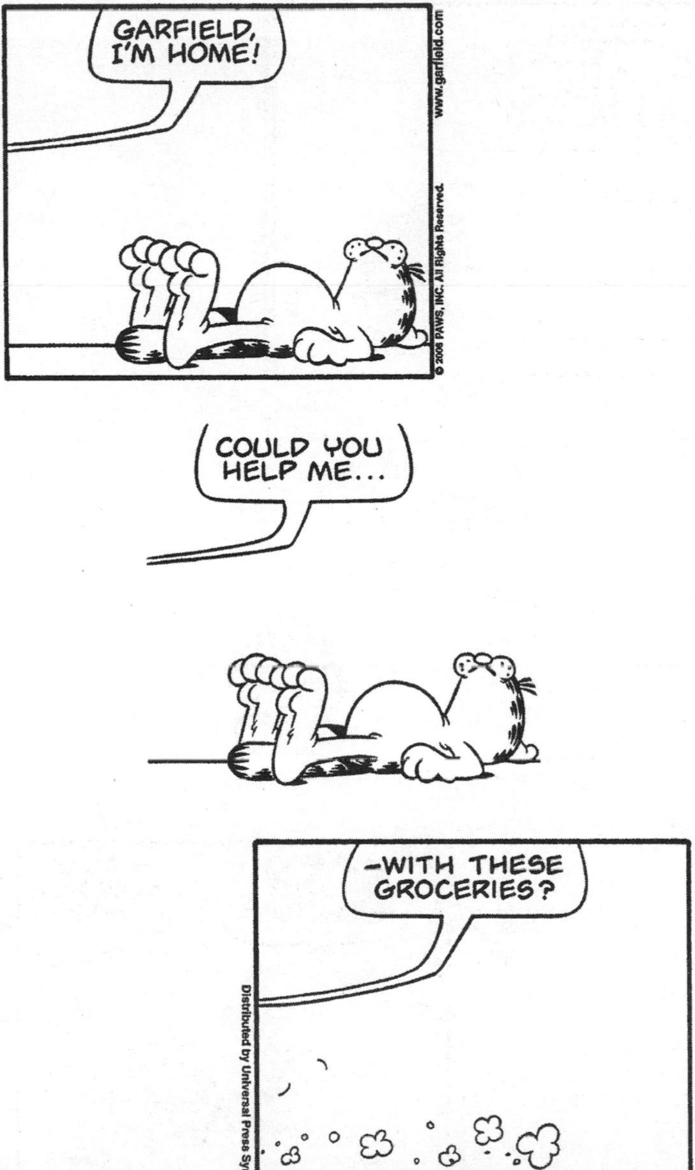
GARFIELD, I'M HOME!
www.garfield.com
© 2006 PAWS, INC. All Rights Reserved.
COULD YOU HELP ME...
-WITH THESE GROCERIES?
Distributed by Universal Press Syndicate
JIM DAVIS 8·3

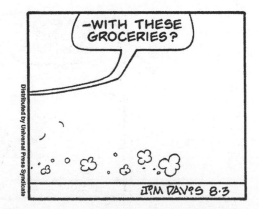

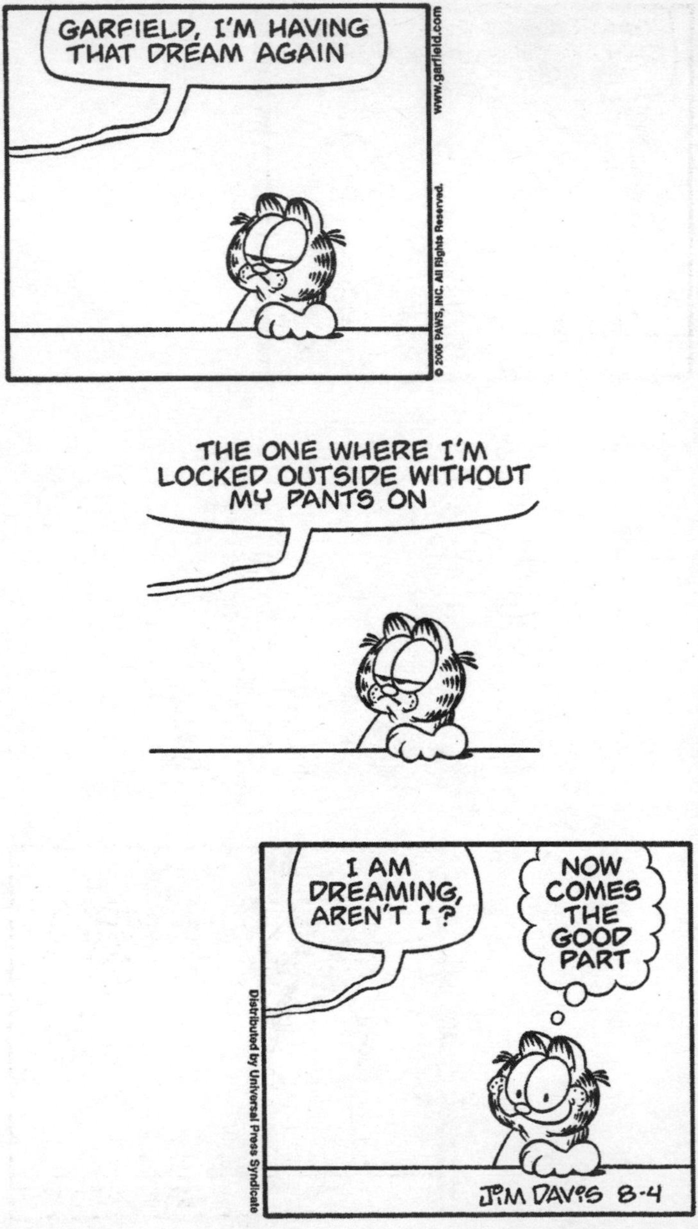
GARFIELD, I'M HAVING THAT DREAM AGAIN
© 2006 PAWS, INC. All Rights Reserved.
www.garfield.com
THE ONE WHERE I'M LOCKED OUTSIDE WITHOUT MY PANTS ON
I AM DREAMING, AREN'T I?
NOW COMES THE GOOD PART
Distributed by Universal Press Syndicate
JIM DAVIS 8-4

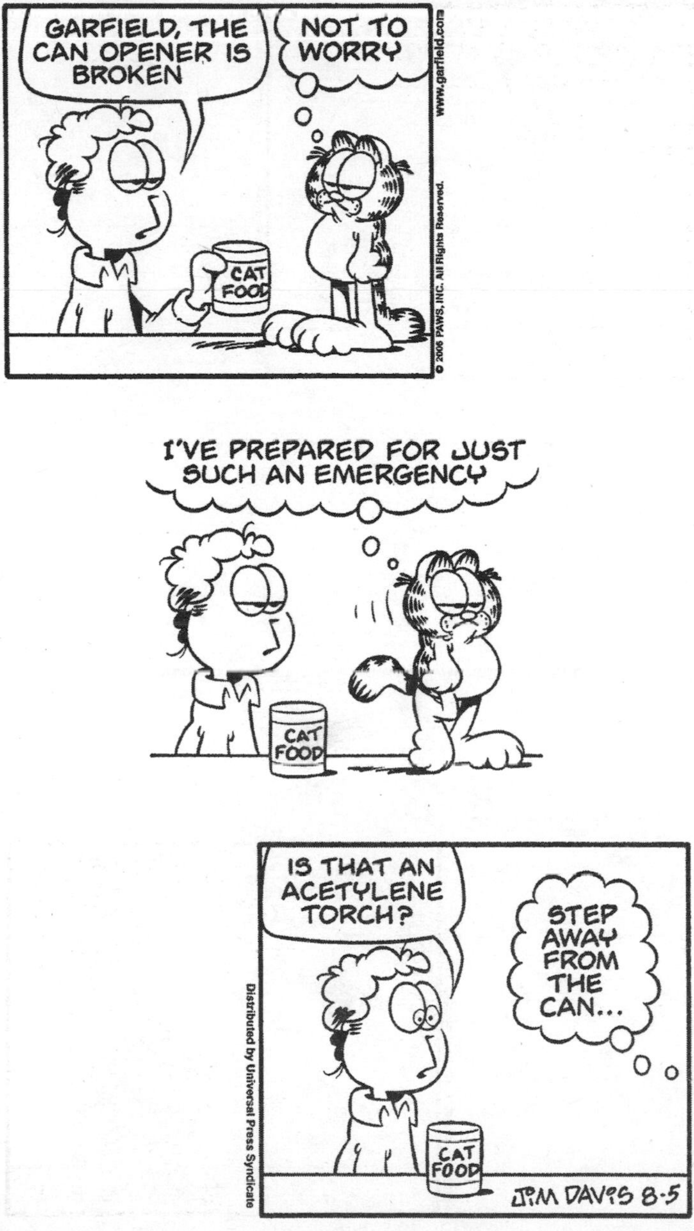
GARFIELD, THE CAN OPENER IS BROKEN
NOT TO WORRY
CAT FOOD
www.garfield.com
© 2006 PAWS, INC. All Rights Reserved.
I'VE PREPARED FOR JUST SUCH AN EMERGENCY
CAT FOOD
IS THAT AN ACETYLENE TORCH?
STEP AWAY FROM THE CAN...
CAT FOOD
JIM DAVIS 8-5
Distributed by Universal Press Syndicate

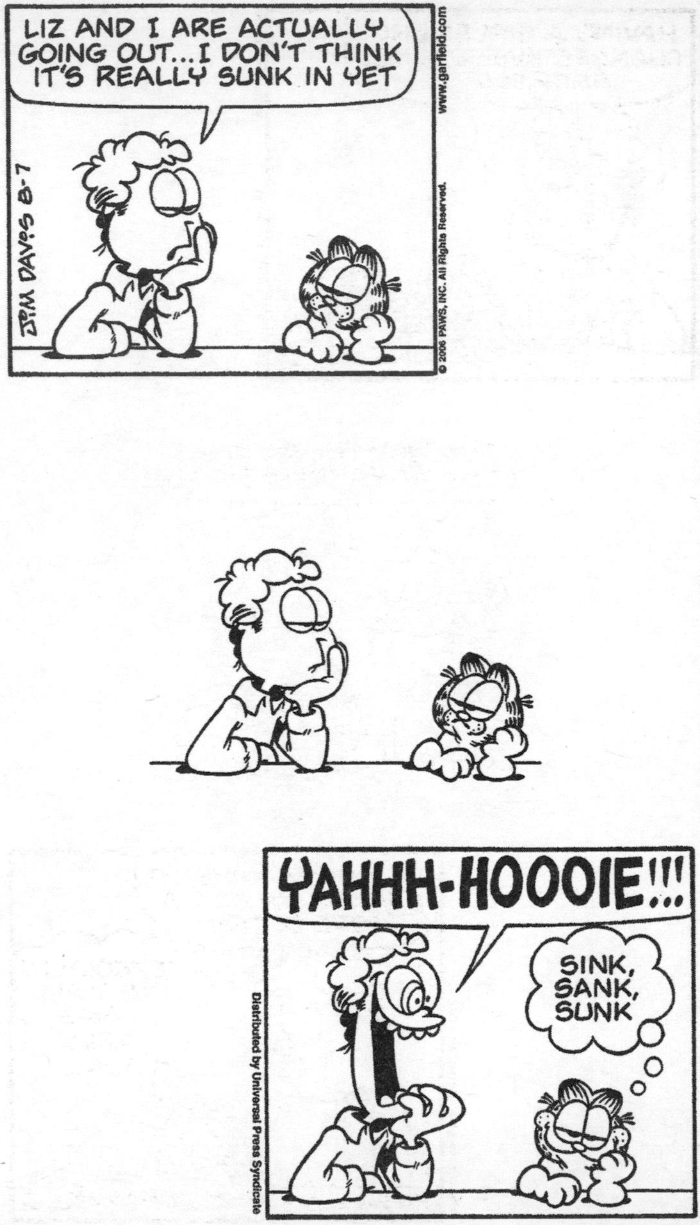
LIZ AND I ARE ACTUALLY GOING OUT...I DON'T THINK IT'S REALLY SUNK IN YET
JPM DAVIS 8-7
www.garfield.com
© 2006 PAWS, INC. All Rights Reserved.
YAHHH-HOOOIE!!!
SINK, SANK, SUNK
Distributed by Universal Press Syndicate

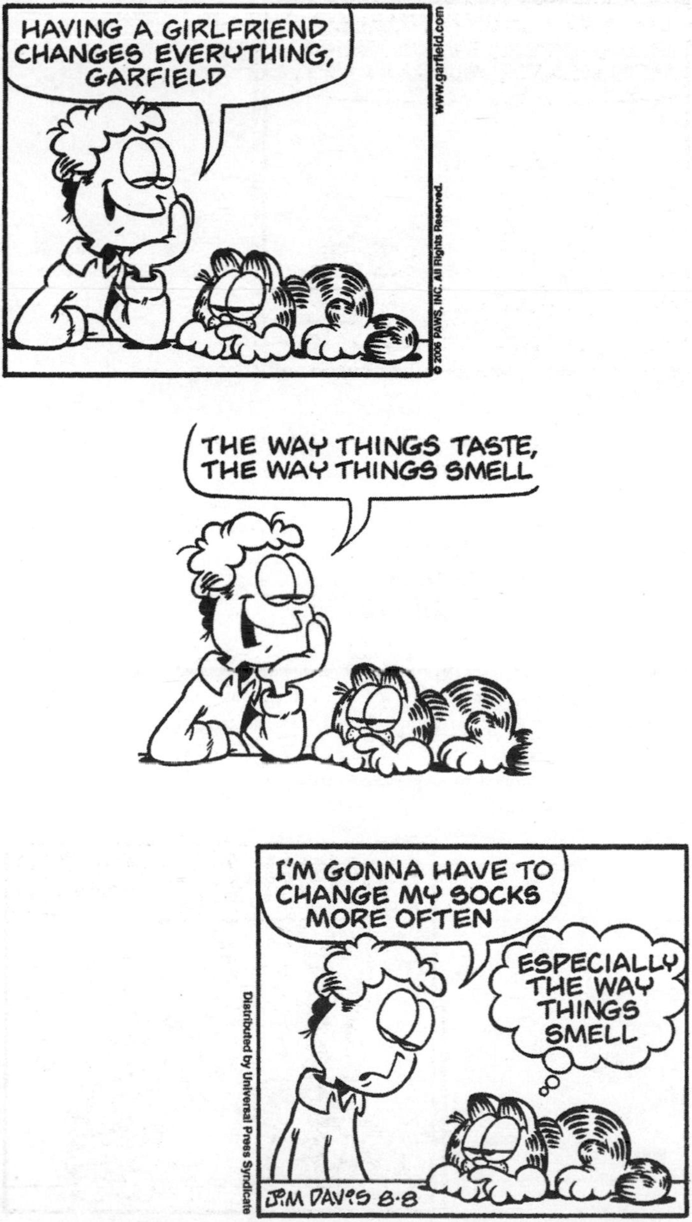
HAVING A GIRLFRIEND CHANGES EVERYTHING, GARFIELD
© 2006 PAWS, INC. All Rights Reserved. www.garfield.com
THE WAY THINGS TASTE, THE WAY THINGS SMELL
I'M GONNA HAVE TO CHANGE MY SOCKS MORE OFTEN
ESPECIALLY THE WAY THINGS SMELL
JIM DAVIS 8·8
Distributed by Universal Press Syndicate

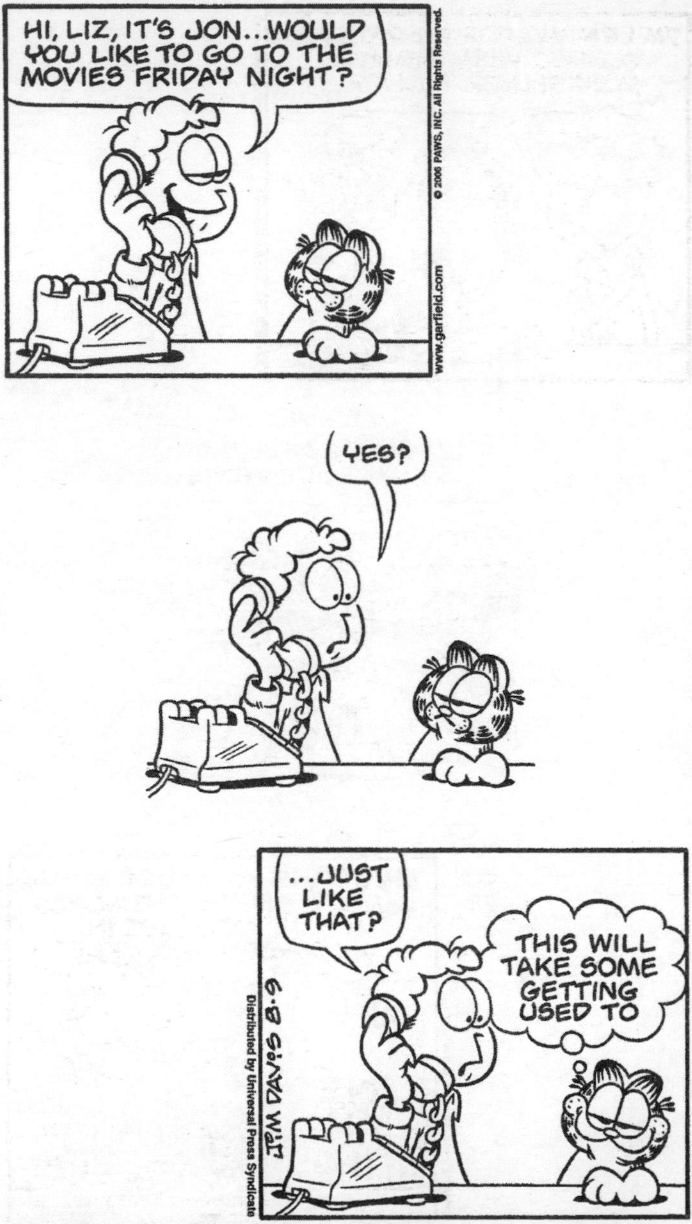
HI, LIZ, IT'S JON...WOULD YOU LIKE TO GO TO THE MOVIES FRIDAY NIGHT?
© 2006 PAWS, INC. All Rights Reserved.
www.garfield.com
YES?
...JUST LIKE THAT?
THIS WILL TAKE SOME GETTING USED TO
JIM DAVIS 8-9
Distributed by Universal Press Syndicate

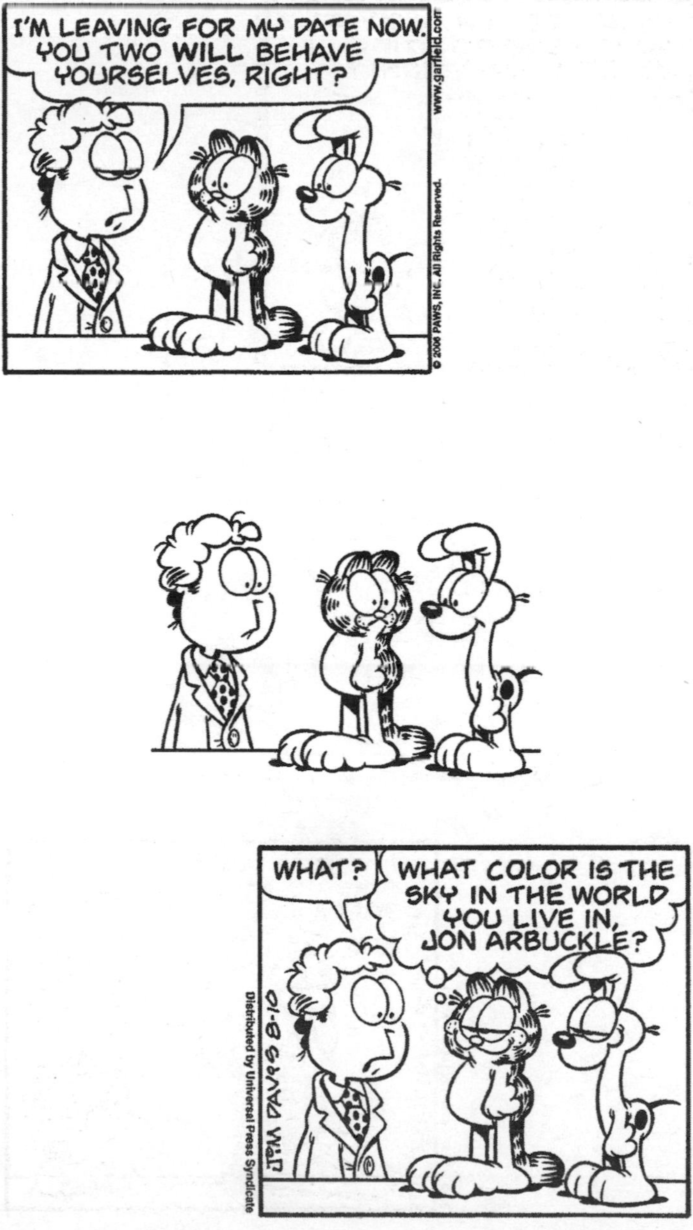
I'M LEAVING FOR MY DATE NOW. YOU TWO WILL BEHAVE YOURSELVES, RIGHT?
© 2006 PAWS, INC. All Rights Reserved.
www.garfield.com
WHAT?
WHAT COLOR IS THE SKY IN THE WORLD YOU LIVE IN, JON ARBUCKLE?
JIM DAVIS 8-10
Distributed by Universal Press Syndicate

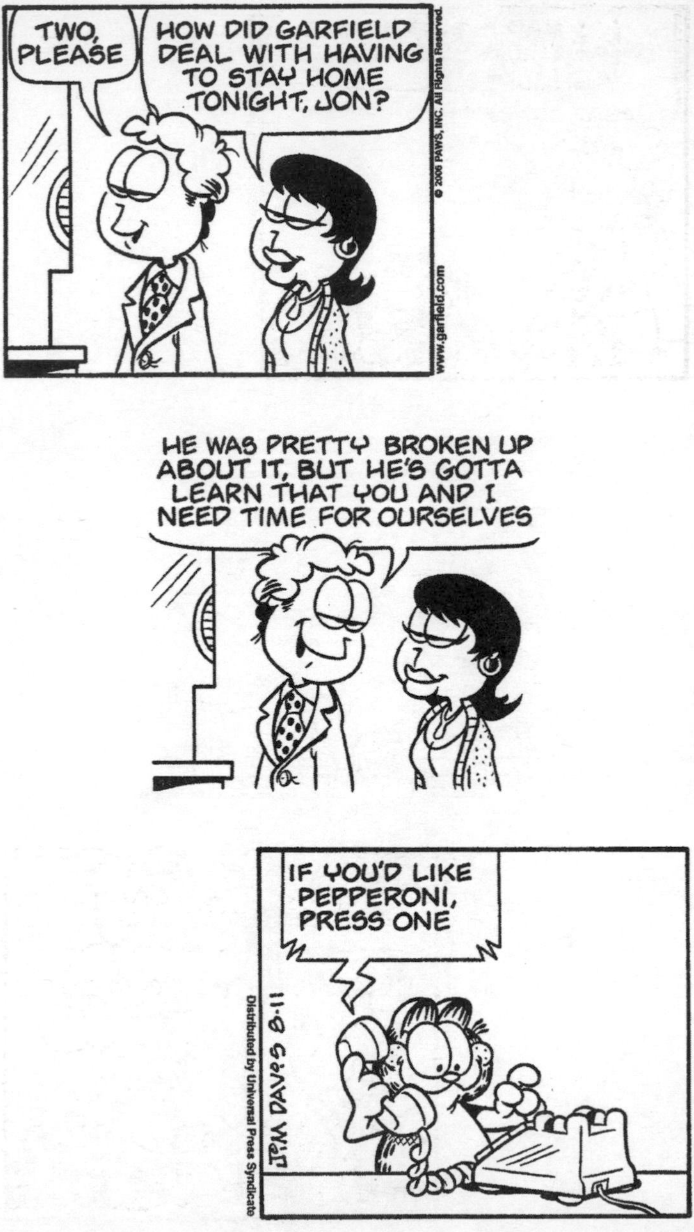
TWO, PLEASE
HOW DID GARFIELD DEAL WITH HAVING TO STAY HOME TONIGHT, JON?
© 2006 PAWS, INC. All Rights Reserved.
www.garfield.com
HE WAS PRETTY BROKEN UP ABOUT IT, BUT HE'S GOTTA LEARN THAT YOU AND I NEED TIME FOR OURSELVES
IF YOU'D LIKE PEPPERONI, PRESS ONE
JIM DAVIS 8-11
Distributed by Universal Press Syndicate

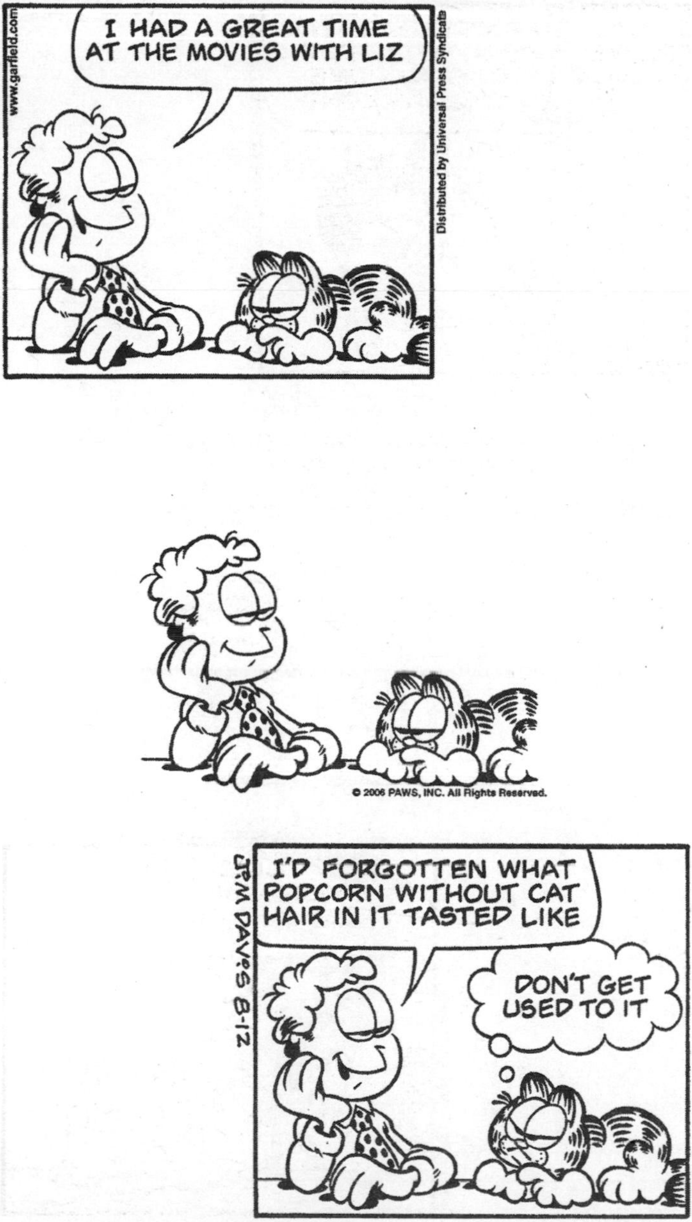
www.garfield.com
I HAD A GREAT TIME AT THE MOVIES WITH LIZ
Distributed by Universal Press Syndicate
© 2006 PAWS, INC. All Rights Reserved.
JPM DAVIS 8-12
I'D FORGOTTEN WHAT POPCORN WITHOUT CAT HAIR IN IT TASTED LIKE
DON'T GET USED TO IT

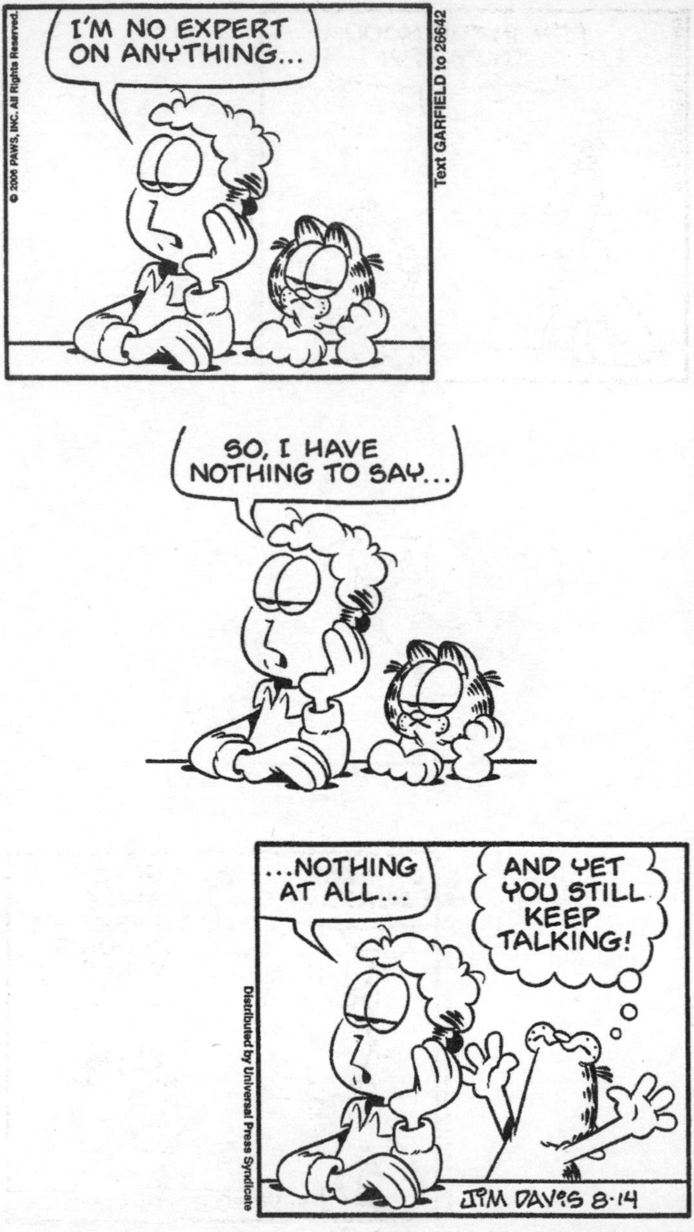
© 2006 PAWS, INC. All Rights Reserved.
Text GARFIELD to 26642
I'M NO EXPERT ON ANYTHING...
SO, I HAVE NOTHING TO SAY...
...NOTHING AT ALL...
AND YET YOU STILL KEEP TALKING!
Distributed by Universal Press Syndicate
JIM DAVIS 8·14

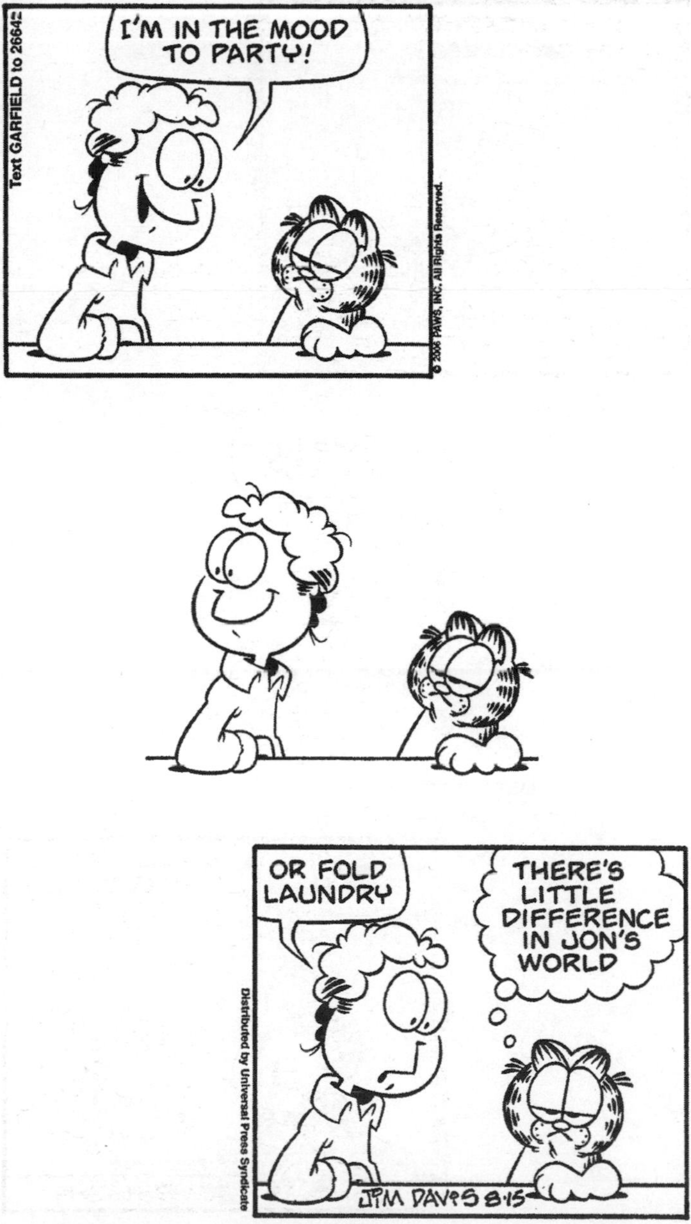
Text GARFIELD to 26642
I'M IN THE MOOD TO PARTY!
OR FOLD LAUNDRY
THERE'S LITTLE DIFFERENCE IN JON'S WORLD
JIM DAVIS 8-15
Distributed by Universal Press Syndicate

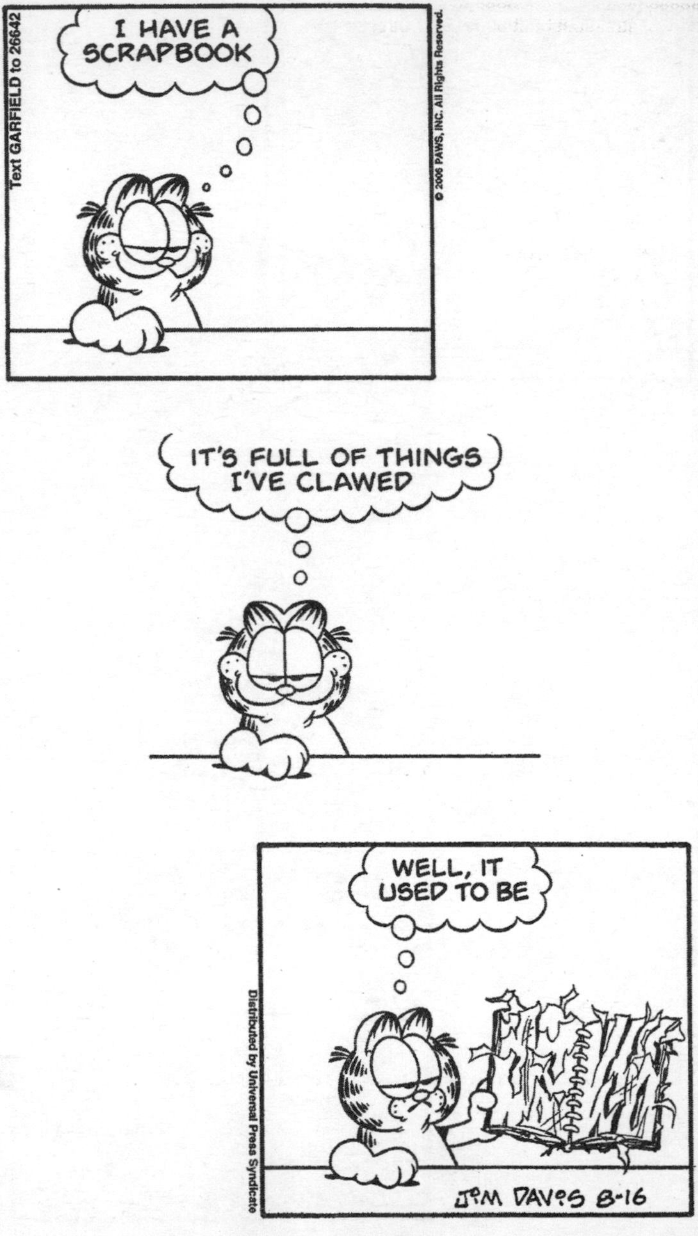
Text GARFIELD to 26642
I HAVE A SCRAPBOOK
© 2006 PAWS, INC. All Rights Reserved.
IT'S FULL OF THINGS I'VE CLAWED
WELL, IT USED TO BE
Distributed by Universal Press Syndicate
JIM DAVIS 8-16

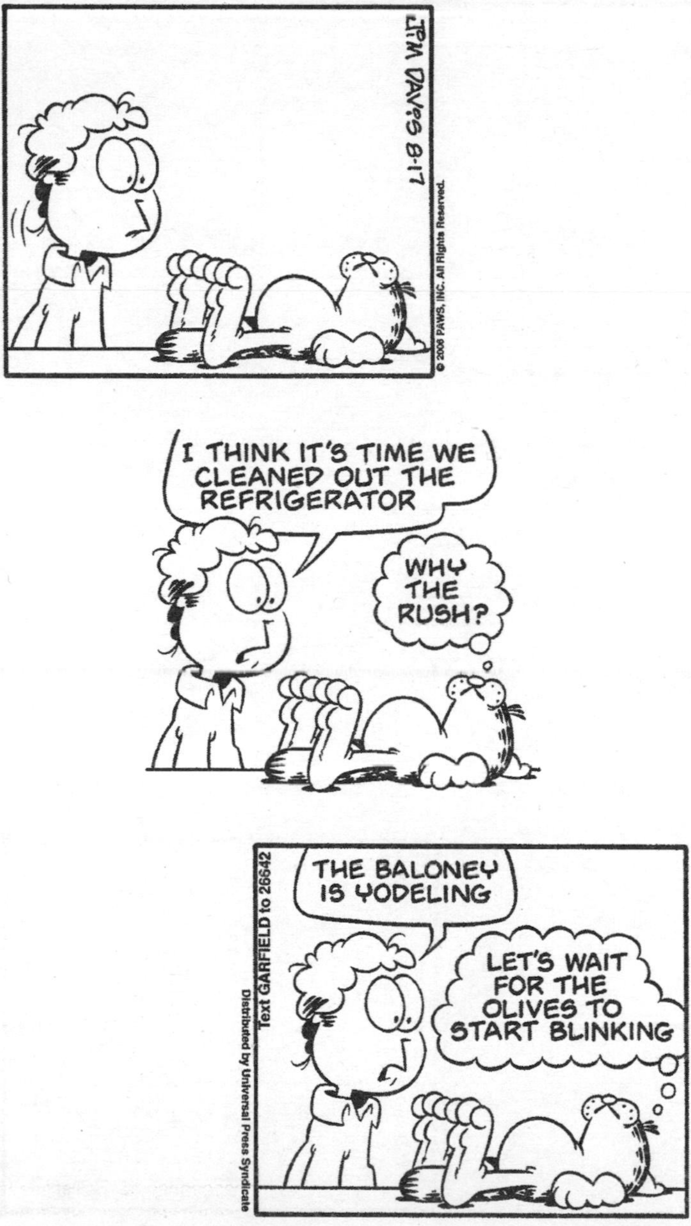

JPM DAVPS 8-17
© 2008 PAWS, INC. All Rights Reserved.
I THINK IT'S TIME WE CLEANED OUT THE REFRIGERATOR
WHY THE RUSH?
THE BALONEY IS YODELING
LET'S WAIT FOR THE OLIVES TO START BLINKING
Text GARFIELD to 26642
Distributed by Universal Press Syndicate

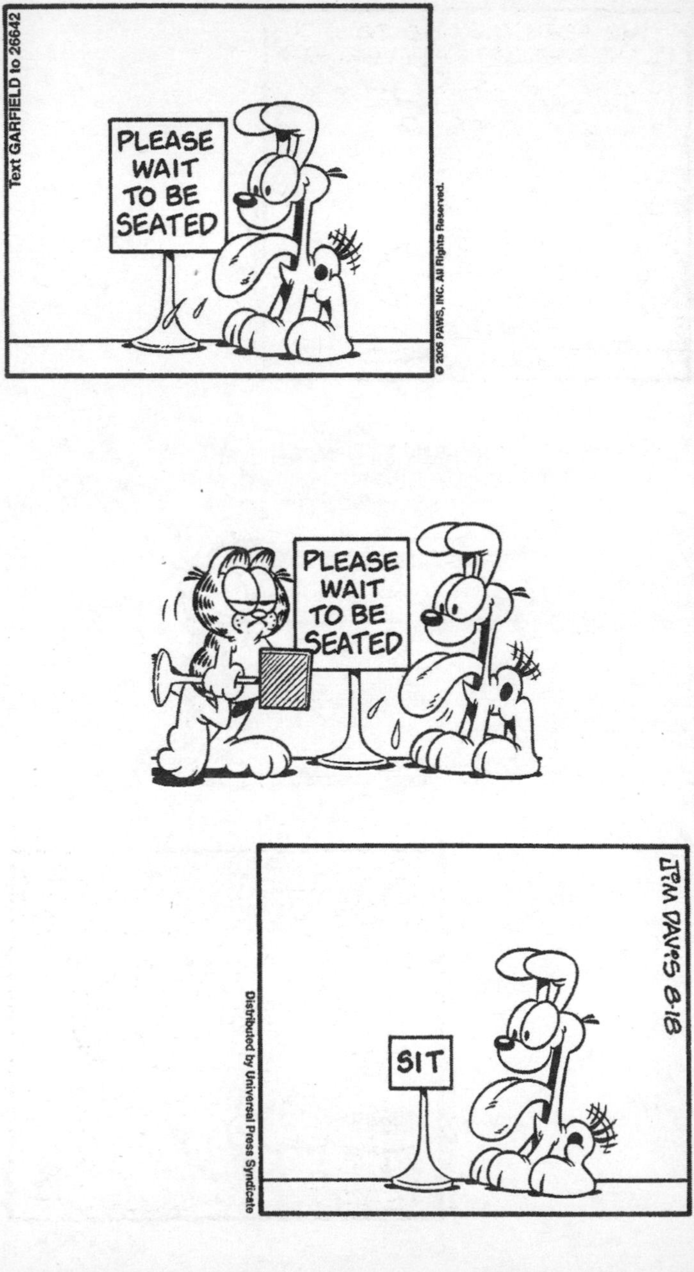
Text GARFIELD to 26642
PLEASE WAIT TO BE SEATED
© 2006 PAWS, INC. All Rights Reserved.
PLEASE WAIT TO BE SEATED
JIM DAVIS 8-18
SIT
Distributed by Universal Press Syndicate

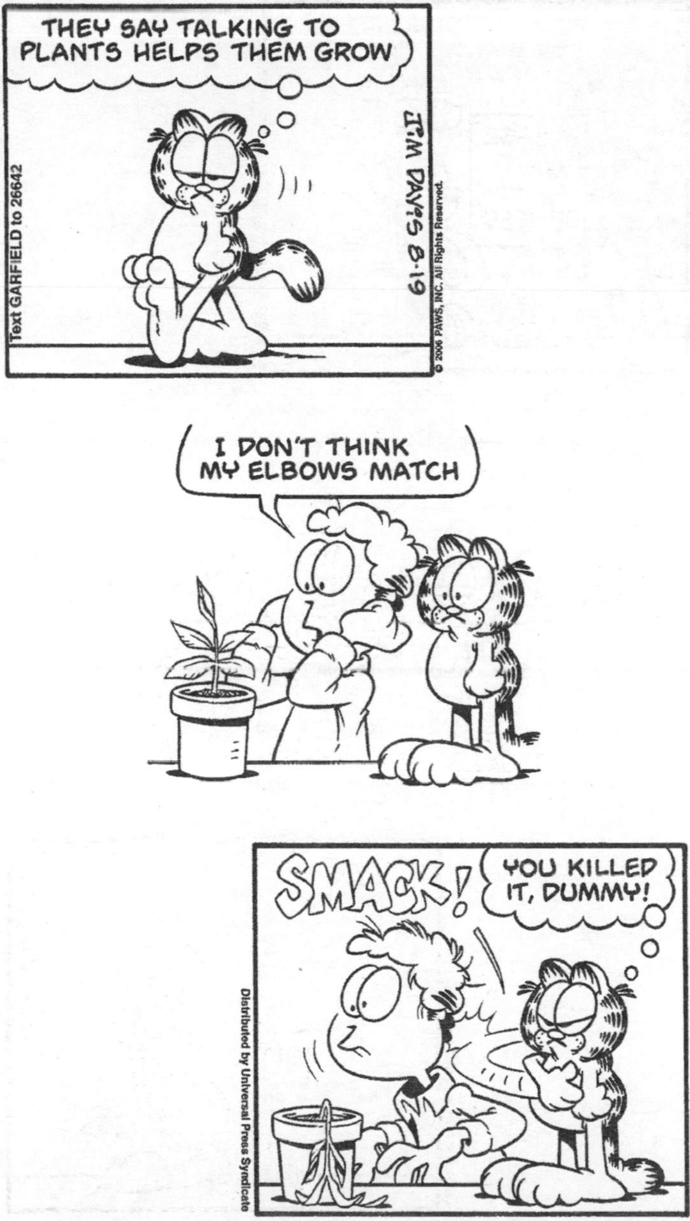
THEY SAY TALKING TO PLANTS HELPS THEM GROW
Text GARFIELD to 26642
JIM DAVIS 8-19
© 2006 PAWS, INC. All Rights Reserved.
I DON'T THINK MY ELBOWS MATCH
SMACK!
YOU KILLED IT, DUMMY!
Distributed by Universal Press Syndicate

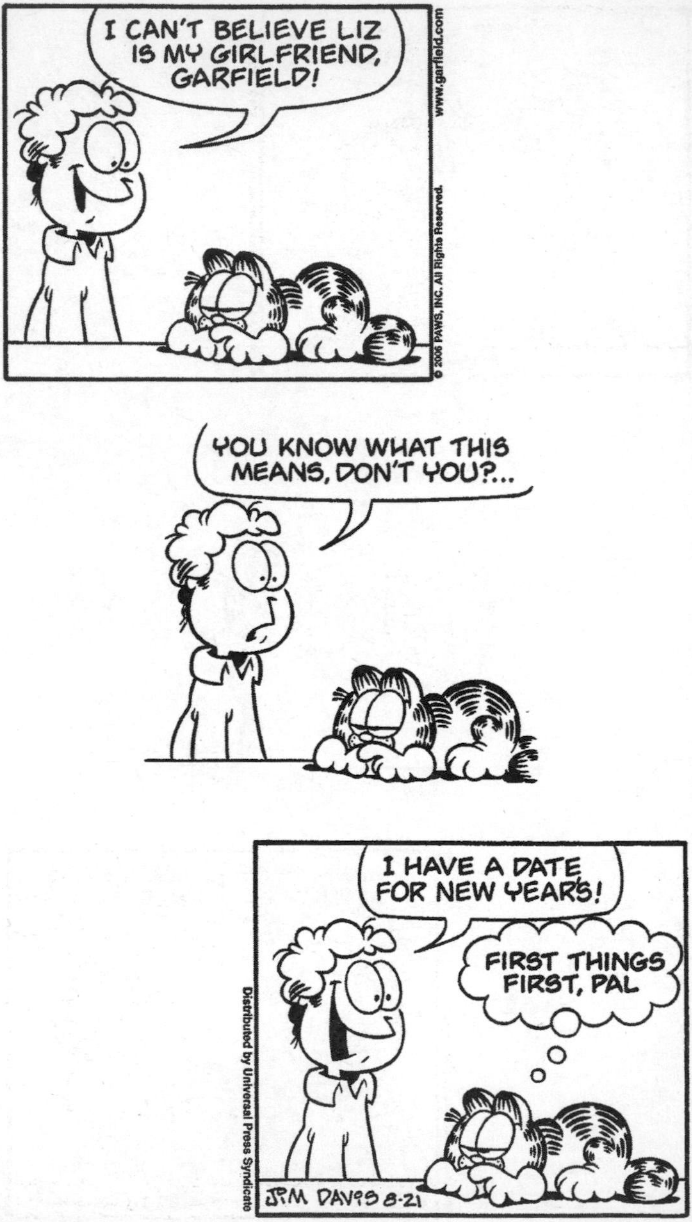
I CAN'T BELIEVE LIZ IS MY GIRLFRIEND, GARFIELD!
© 2006 PAWS, INC. All Rights Reserved. www.garfield.com
YOU KNOW WHAT THIS MEANS, DON'T YOU?...
I HAVE A DATE FOR NEW YEAR'S!
FIRST THINGS FIRST, PAL
Distributed by Universal Press Syndicate
JIM DAVIS 8-21

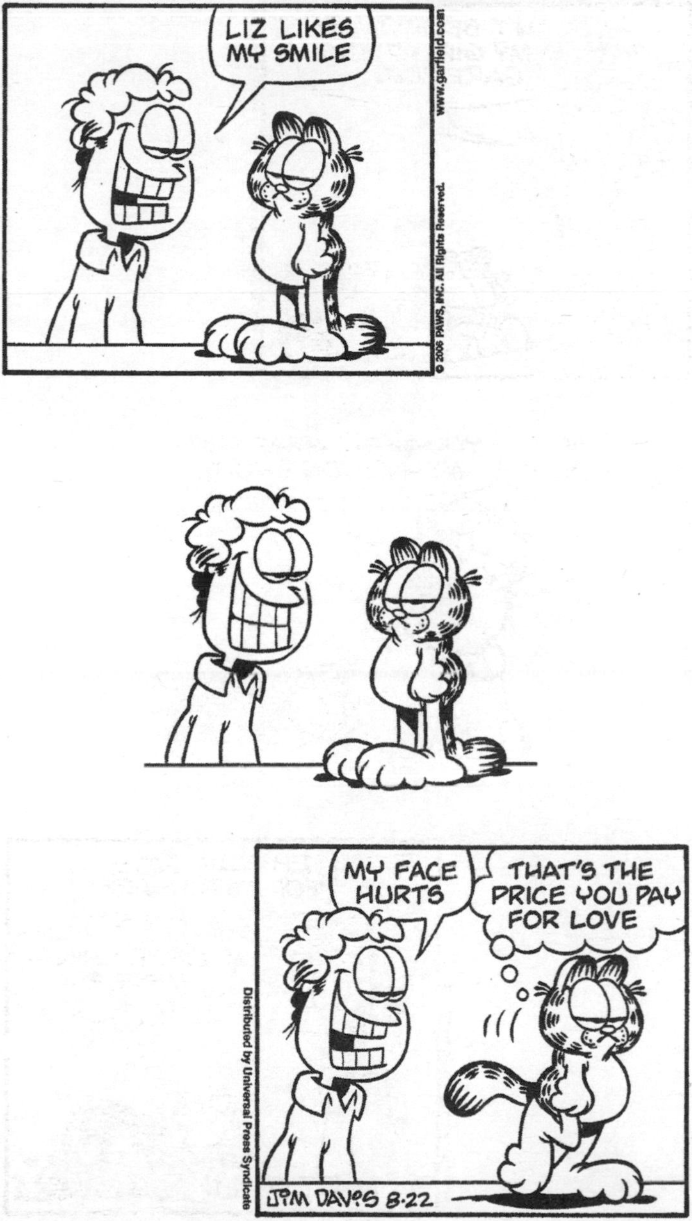
LIZ LIKES MY SMILE
www.garfield.com
© 2006 PAWS, INC. All Rights Reserved.
MY FACE HURTS
THAT'S THE PRICE YOU PAY FOR LOVE
Distributed by Universal Press Syndicate
JIM DAVIS 8-22

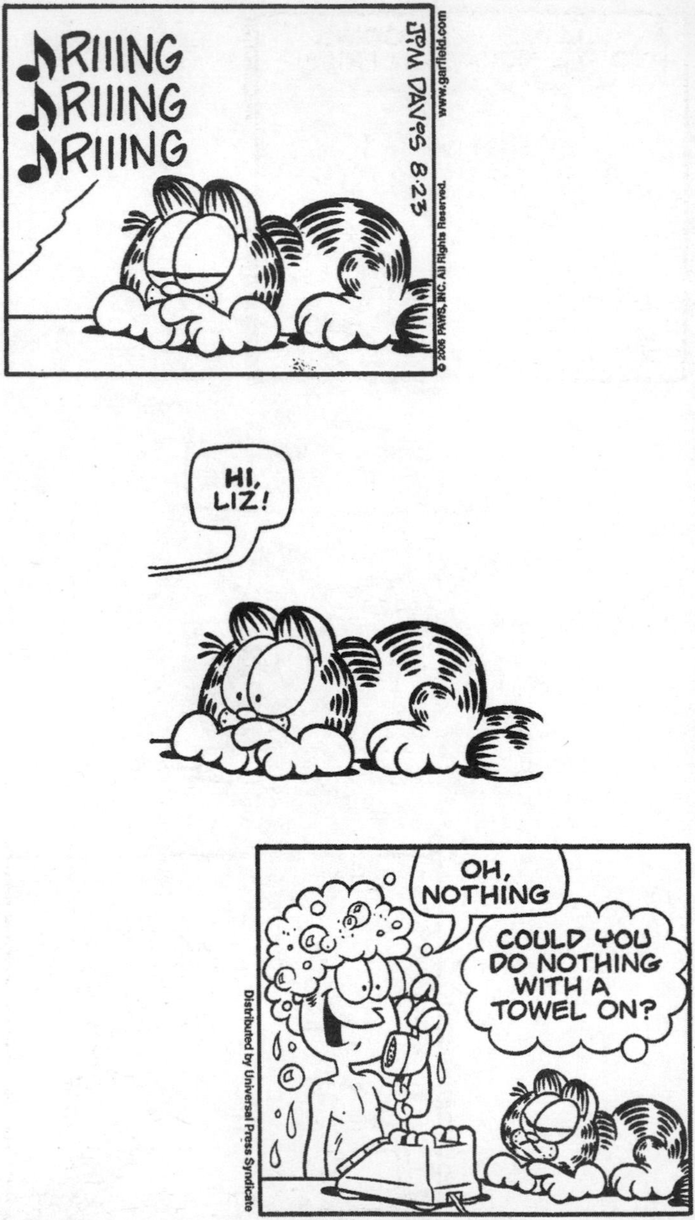
RIIING
RIIING
RIIING
JPM DAVIS 8·23
www.garfield.com
© 2006 PAWS, INC. All Rights Reserved.
HI, LIZ!
OH, NOTHING
COULD YOU DO NOTHING WITH A TOWEL ON?
Distributed by Universal Press Syndicate

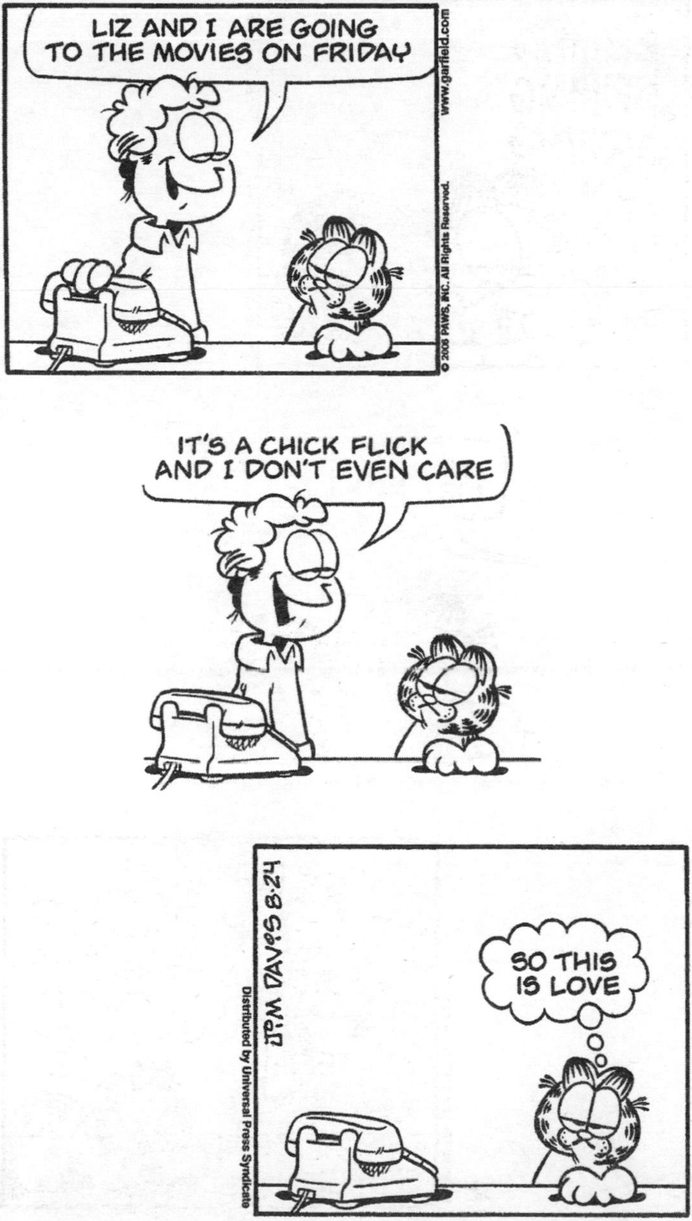
LIZ AND I ARE GOING TO THE MOVIES ON FRIDAY
© 2006 PAWS, INC. All Rights Reserved.
www.garfield.com
IT'S A CHICK FLICK AND I DON'T EVEN CARE
JIM DAVIS 8·24
Distributed by Universal Press Syndicate
SO THIS IS LOVE

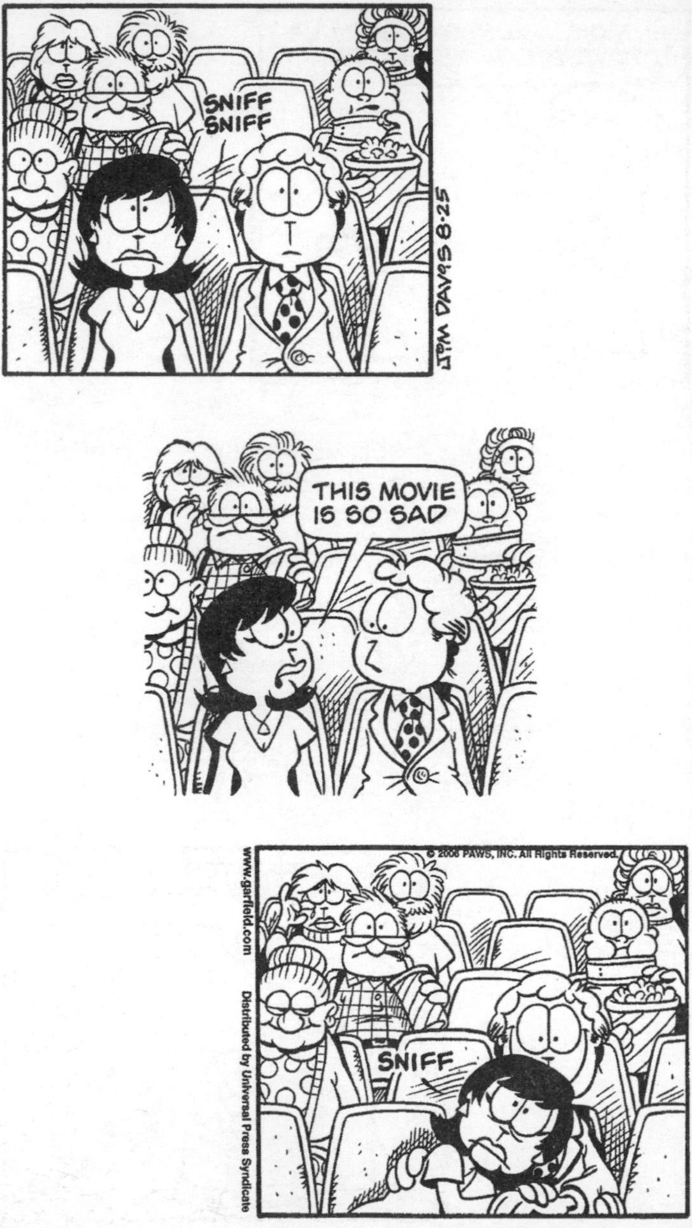
SNIFF
SNIFF
JPM DAVIS 8-25
THIS MOVIE IS SO SAD
© 2006 PAWS, INC. All Rights Reserved.
www.garfield.com
Distributed by Universal Press Syndicate
SNIFF

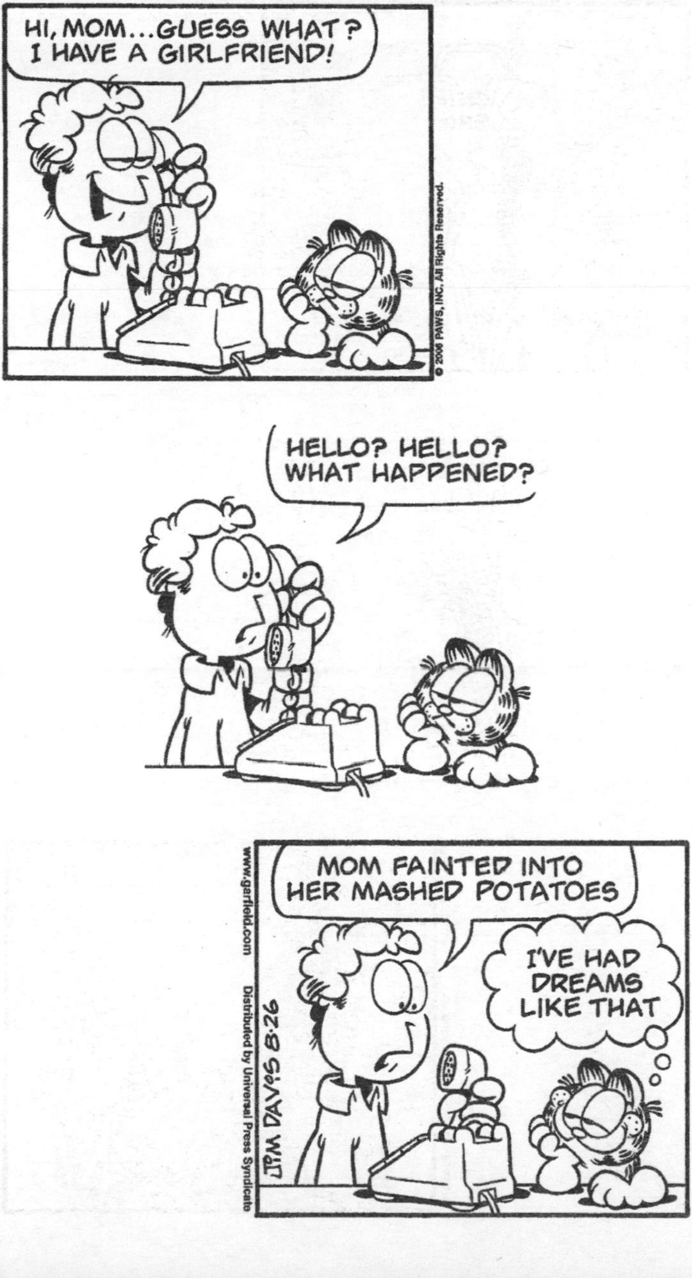
HI, MOM...GUESS WHAT? I HAVE A GIRLFRIEND!
© 2006 PAWS, INC. All Rights Reserved.
HELLO? HELLO? WHAT HAPPENED?
www.garfield.com
Distributed by Universal Press Syndicate
JIM DAVIS 8-26
MOM FAINTED INTO HER MASHED POTATOES
I'VE HAD DREAMS LIKE THAT

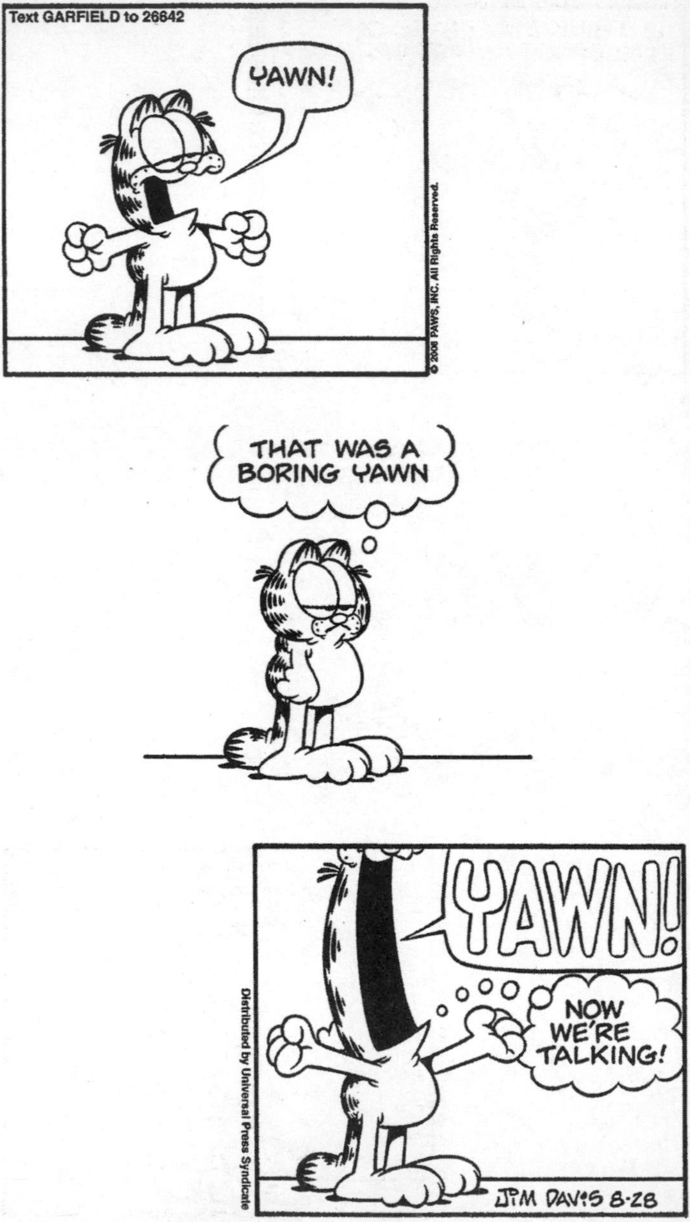
Text GARFIELD to 26642
YAWN!
© 2006 PAWS, INC. All Rights Reserved.
THAT WAS A BORING YAWN
YAWN!
NOW WE'RE TALKING!
Distributed by Universal Press Syndicate
JIM DAVIS 8-28

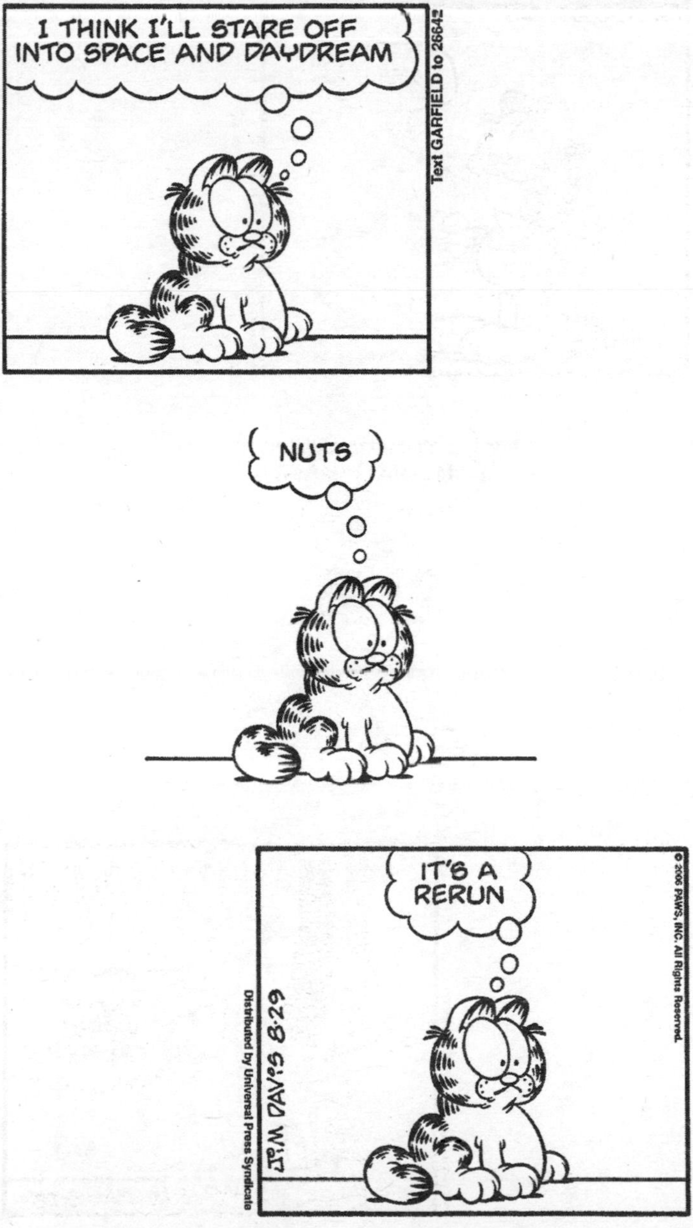
I THINK I'LL STARE OFF INTO SPACE AND DAYDREAM
Text GARFIELD to 26642
NUTS
IT'S A RERUN
© 2006 PAWS, INC. All Rights Reserved.
JIM DAVIS 8·29
Distributed by Universal Press Syndicate

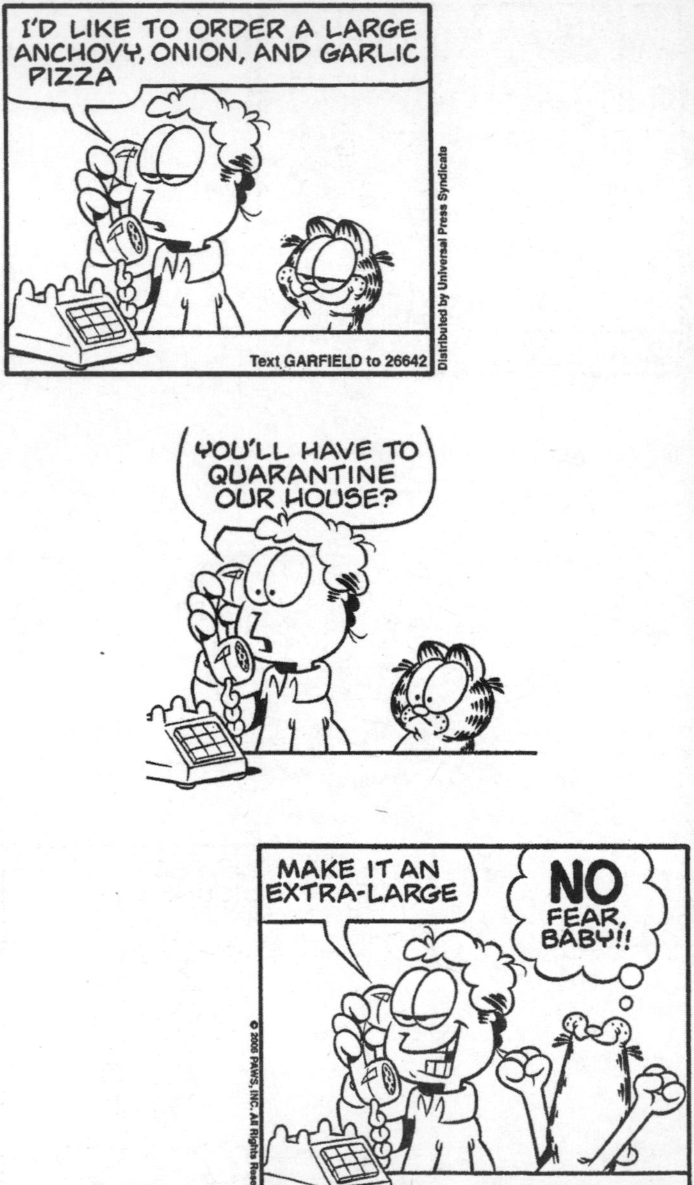
I'D LIKE TO ORDER A LARGE ANCHOVY, ONION, AND GARLIC PIZZA
Text GARFIELD to 26642
Distributed by Universal Press Syndicate
YOU'LL HAVE TO QUARANTINE OUR HOUSE?
MAKE IT AN EXTRA-LARGE
NO FEAR, BABY!!
© 2006 PAWS, INC. All Rights Reserved.
JIM DAVIS 8-30

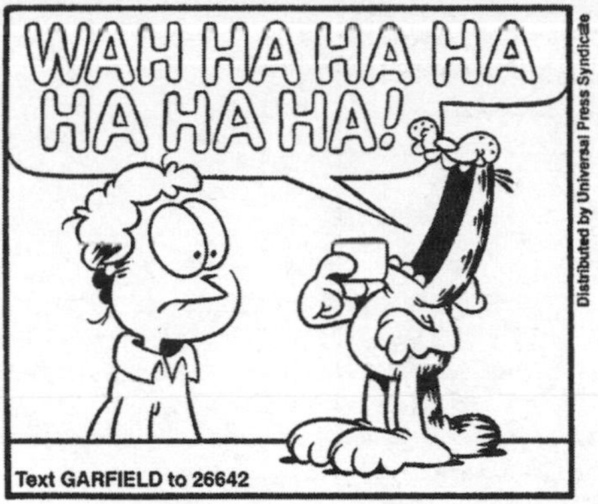
WAH HA HA HA HA HA HA HA!
Text GARFIELD to 26642
Distributed by Universal Press Syndicate

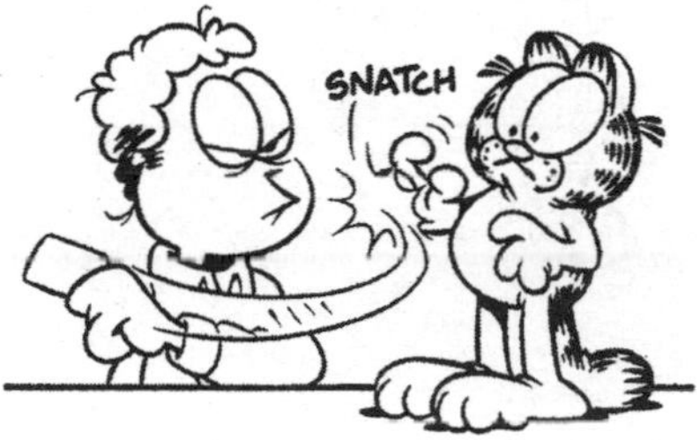
SNATCH

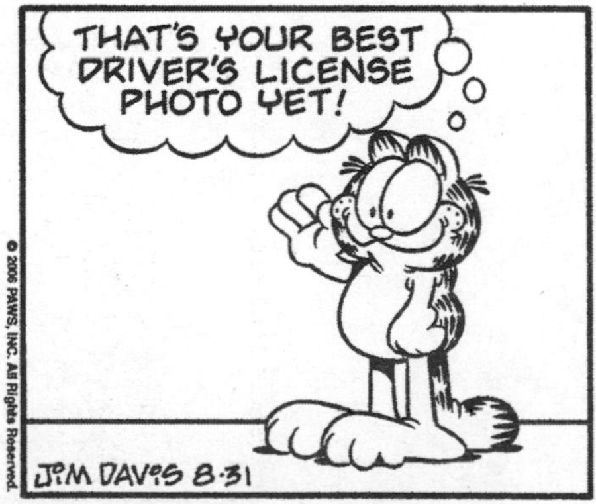
THAT'S YOUR BEST DRIVER'S LICENSE PHOTO YET!
© 2006 PAWS, INC. All Rights Reserved.
JIM DAVIS 8-31

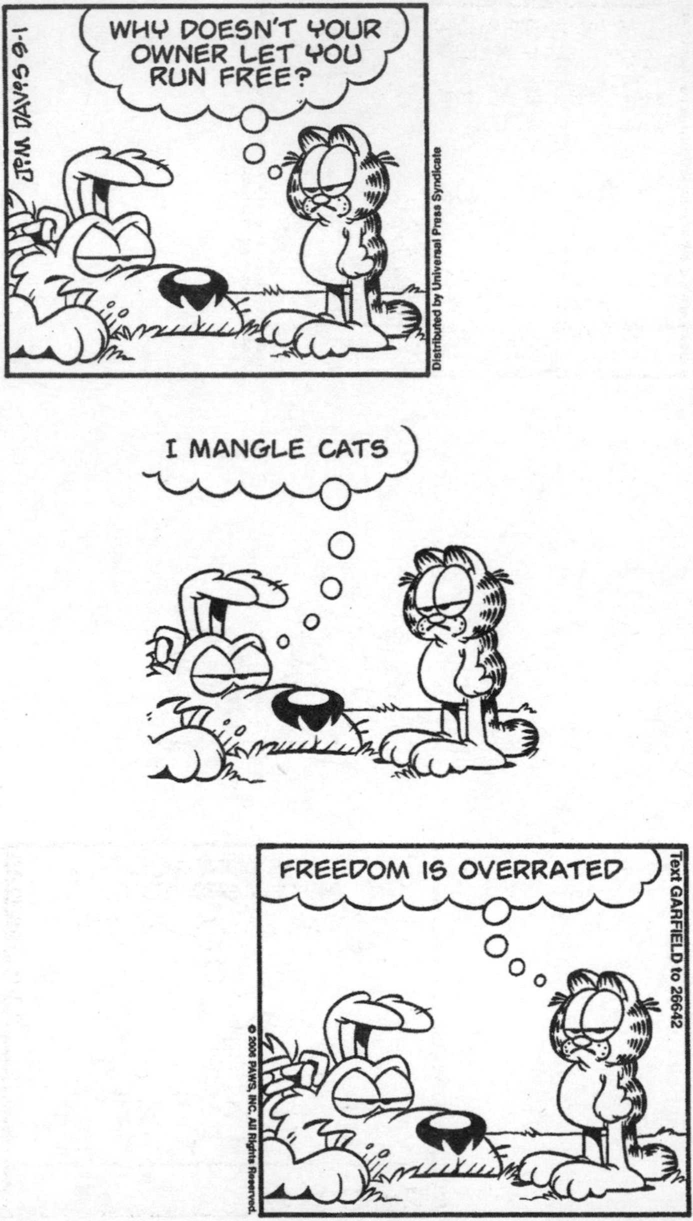
JIM DAVIS 9-1
WHY DOESN'T YOUR OWNER LET YOU RUN FREE?
Distributed by Universal Press Syndicate
I MANGLE CATS
FREEDOM IS OVERRATED
Text GARFIELD to 26642
© 2006 PAWS, INC. All Rights Reserved.

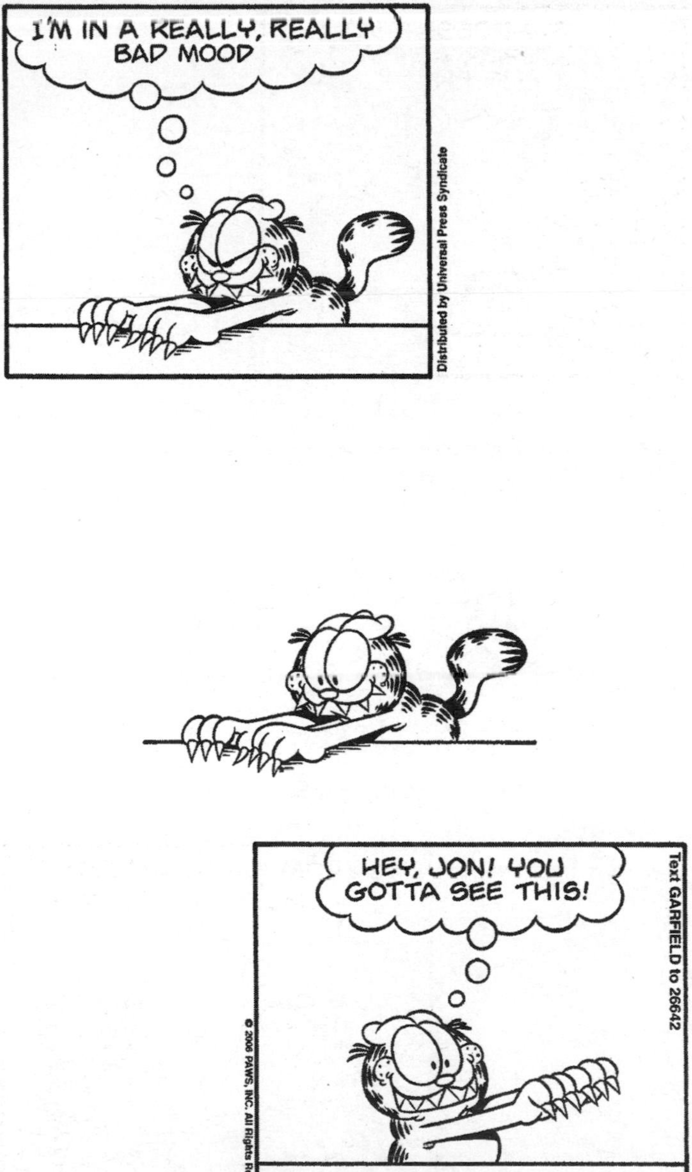
I'M IN A REALLY, REALLY BAD MOOD
Distributed by Universal Press Syndicate
HEY, JON! YOU GOTTA SEE THIS!
Text GARFIELD to 26642
© 2006 PAWS, INC. All Rights Reserved.
JIM DAVIS 9.2

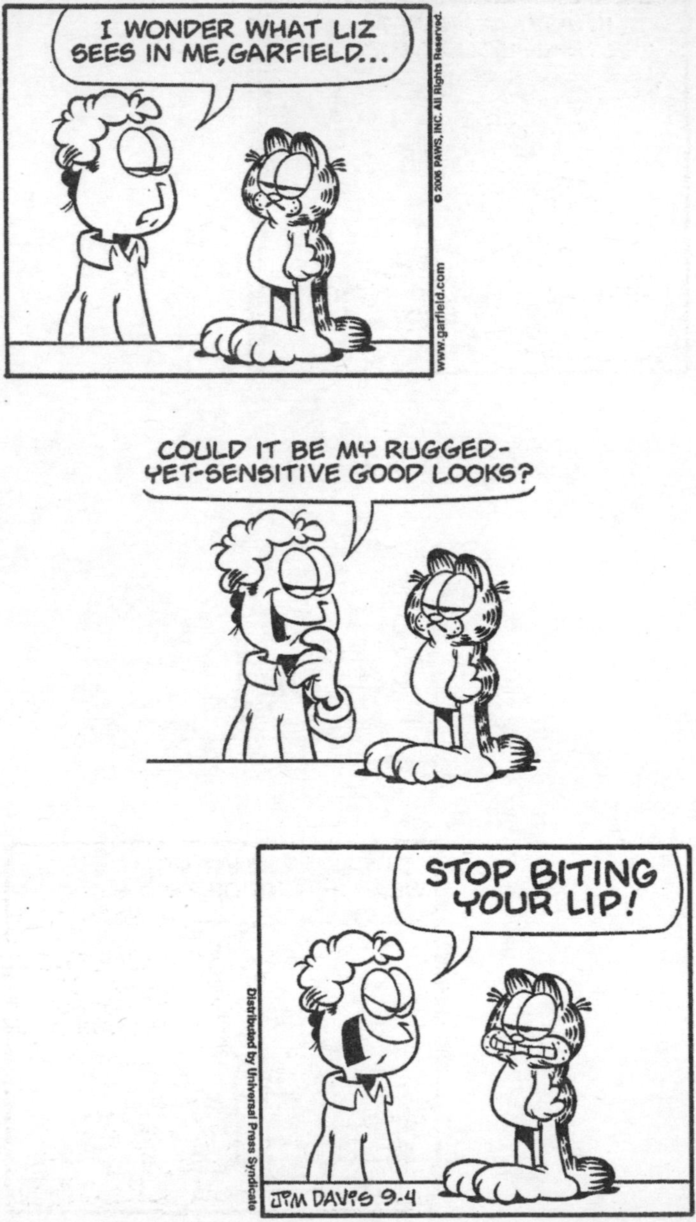
I WONDER WHAT LIZ SEES IN ME, GARFIELD...
© 2006 PAWS, INC. All Rights Reserved.
www.garfield.com
COULD IT BE MY RUGGED-YET-SENSITIVE GOOD LOOKS?
STOP BITING YOUR LIP!
Distributed by Universal Press Syndicate
JIM DAVIS 9-4

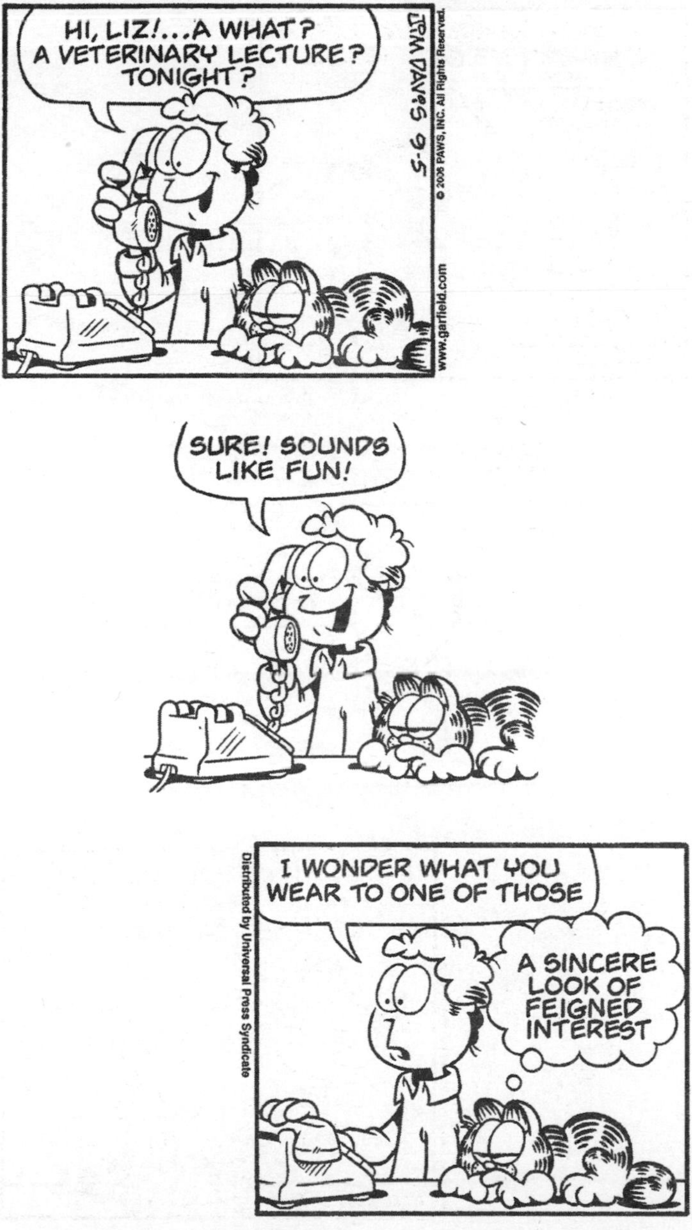
HI, LIZ!...A WHAT? A VETERINARY LECTURE? TONIGHT?
SURE! SOUNDS LIKE FUN!
I WONDER WHAT YOU WEAR TO ONE OF THOSE
A SINCERE LOOK OF FEIGNED INTEREST

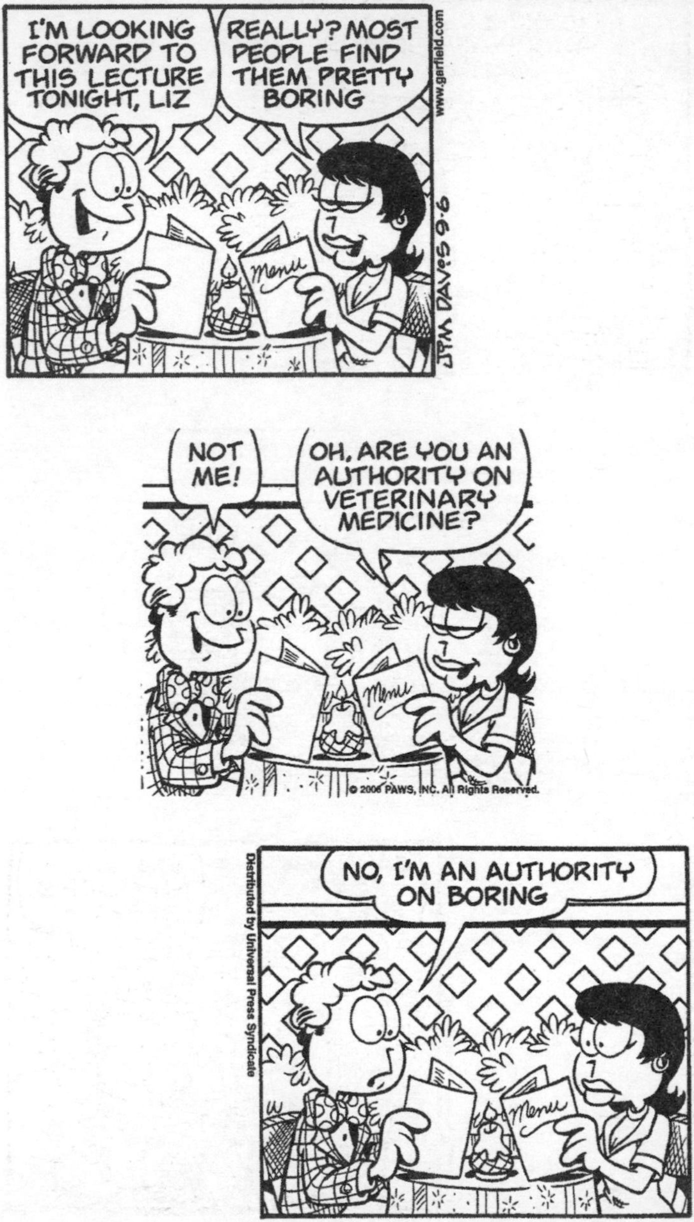
I'M LOOKING FORWARD TO THIS LECTURE TONIGHT, LIZ
REALLY? MOST PEOPLE FIND THEM PRETTY BORING
www.garfield.com
JPM DAVIS 9-6
Menu
NOT ME!
OH, ARE YOU AN AUTHORITY ON VETERINARY MEDICINE?
Menu
© 2006 PAWS, INC. All Rights Reserved.
Distributed by Universal Press Syndicate
NO, I'M AN AUTHORITY ON BORING
Menu

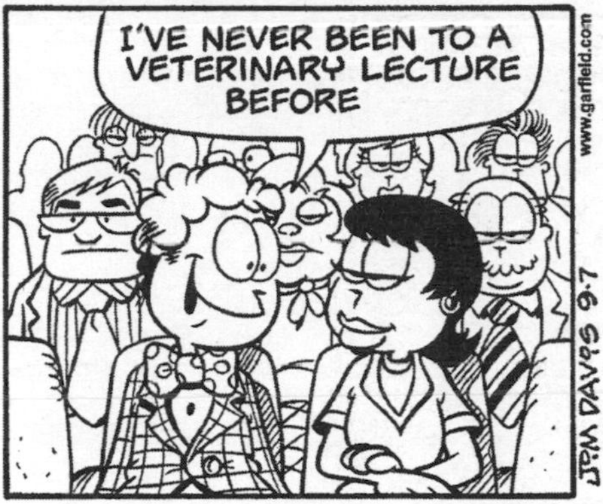
I'VE NEVER BEEN TO A VETERINARY LECTURE BEFORE
www.garfield.com
JIM DAVIS 9·7

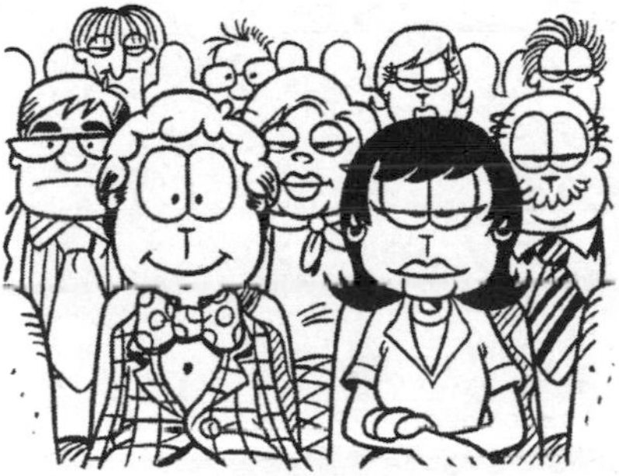

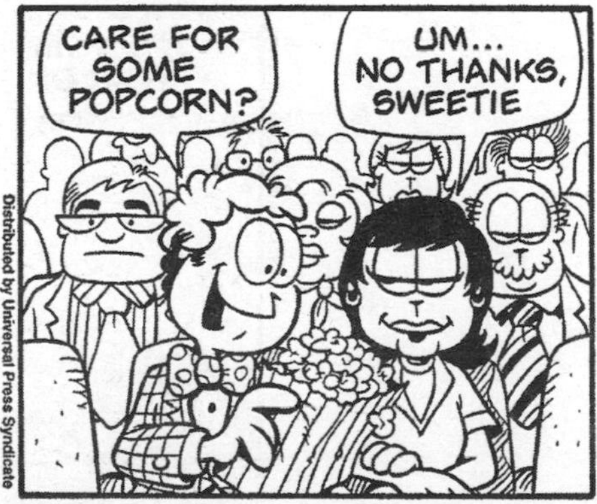
CARE FOR SOME POPCORN?
UM... NO THANKS, SWEETIE
Distributed by Universal Press Syndicate

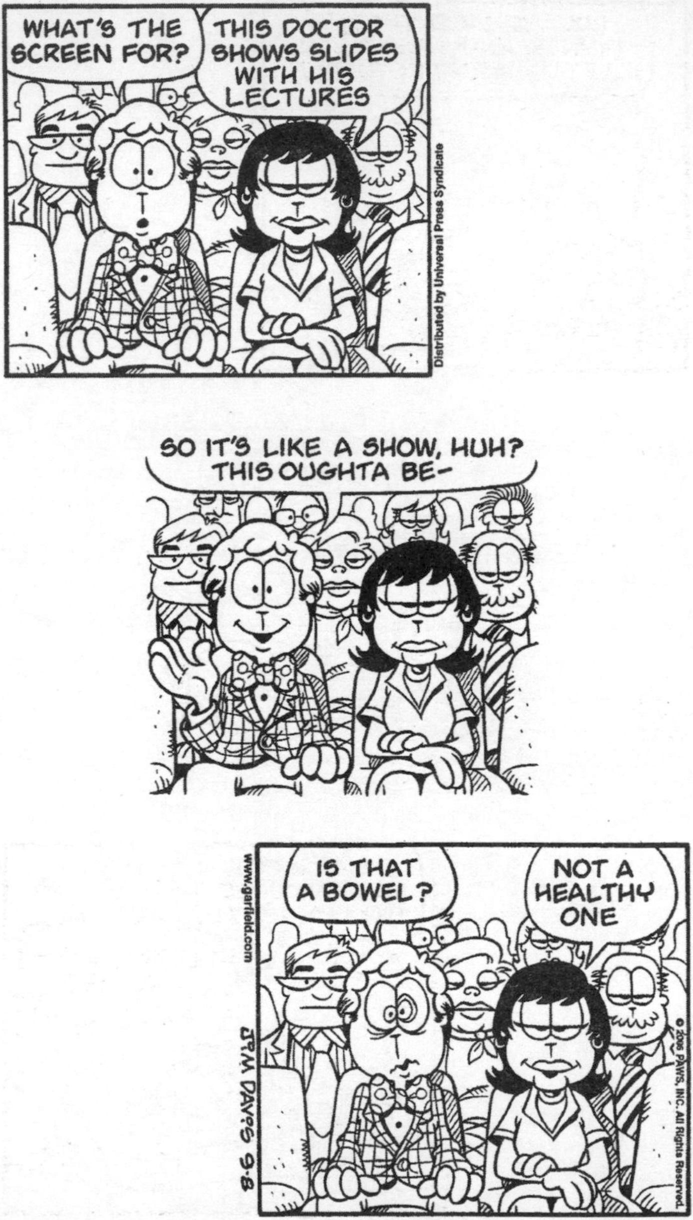
WHAT'S THE SCREEN FOR?
THIS DOCTOR SHOWS SLIDES WITH HIS LECTURES
Distributed by Universal Press Syndicate
SO IT'S LIKE A SHOW, HUH? THIS OUGHTA BE-
IS THAT A BOWEL?
NOT A HEALTHY ONE
www.garfield.com
JIM DAVIS 9-8
© 2006 PAWS, INC. All Rights Reserved.

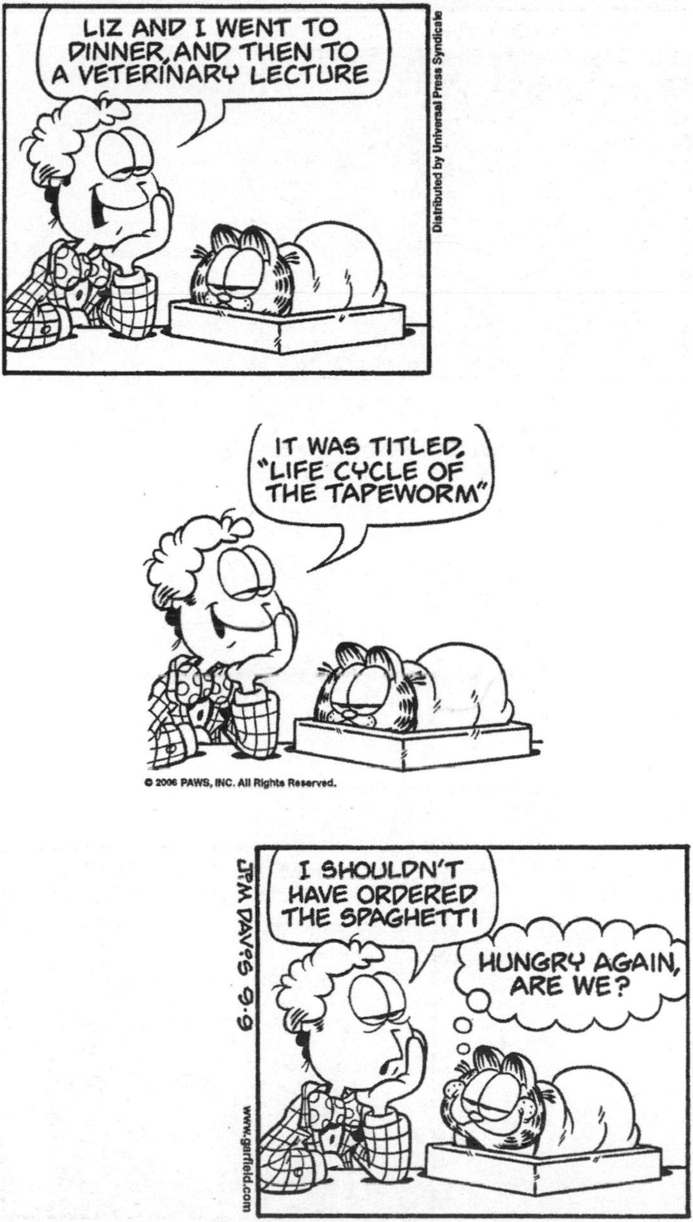
LIZ AND I WENT TO DINNER, AND THEN TO A VETERINARY LECTURE
Distributed by Universal Press Syndicate
IT WAS TITLED, "LIFE CYCLE OF THE TAPEWORM"
I SHOULDN'T HAVE ORDERED THE SPAGHETTI
HUNGRY AGAIN, ARE WE?
JIM DAVIS 9-9
www.garfield.com

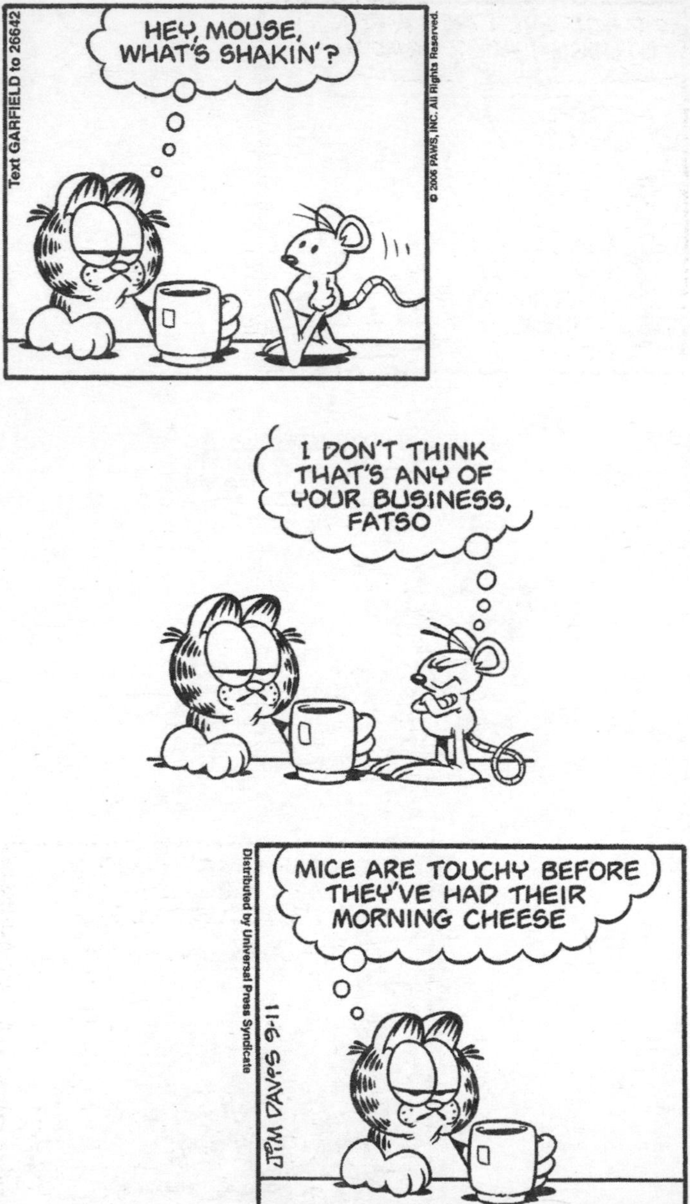
Text GARFIELD to 26642
HEY, MOUSE, WHAT'S SHAKIN'?
© 2006 PAWS, INC. All Rights Reserved.
I DON'T THINK THAT'S ANY OF YOUR BUSINESS, FATSO
Distributed by Universal Press Syndicate
JIM DAVIS 9-11
MICE ARE TOUCHY BEFORE THEY'VE HAD THEIR MORNING CHEESE

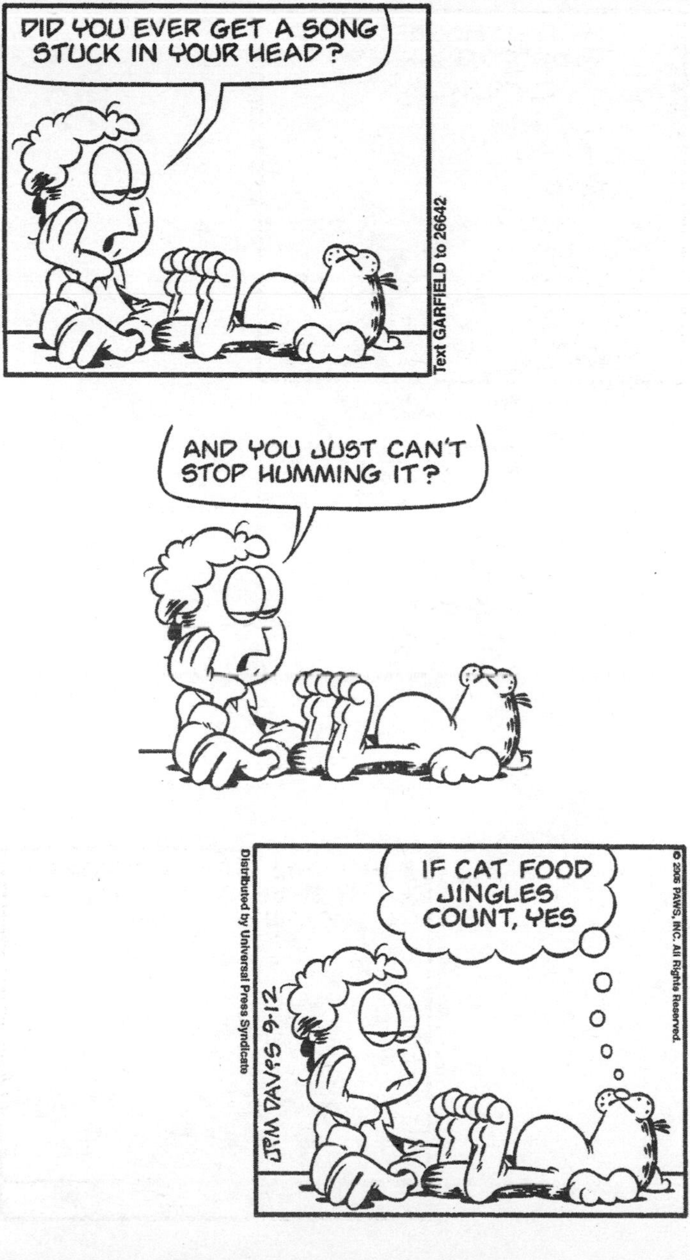
DID YOU EVER GET A SONG STUCK IN YOUR HEAD?
Text GARFIELD to 26642
AND YOU JUST CAN'T STOP HUMMING IT?
IF CAT FOOD JINGLES COUNT, YES
JIM DAVIS 9-12
Distributed by Universal Press Syndicate
© 2005 PAWS, INC. All Rights Reserved.

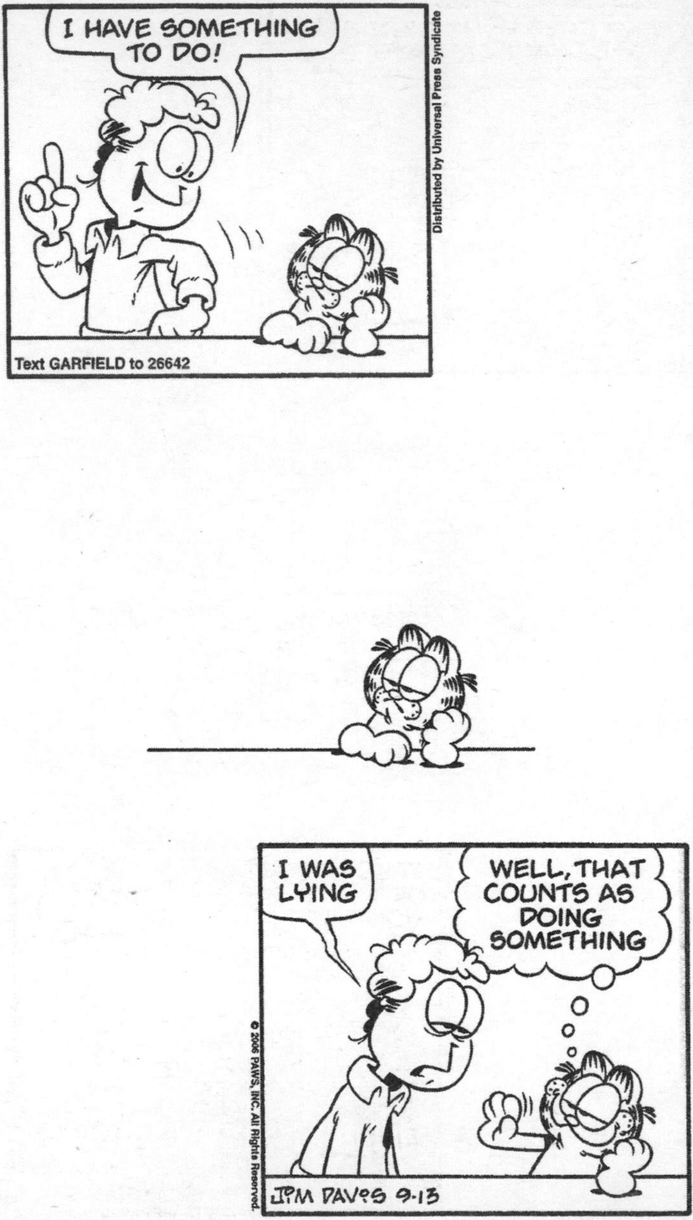
I HAVE SOMETHING TO DO!
Text GARFIELD to 26642
Distributed by Universal Press Syndicate
I WAS LYING
WELL, THAT COUNTS AS DOING SOMETHING
© 2006 PAWS, INC. All Rights Reserved.
JIM DAVIS 9-13

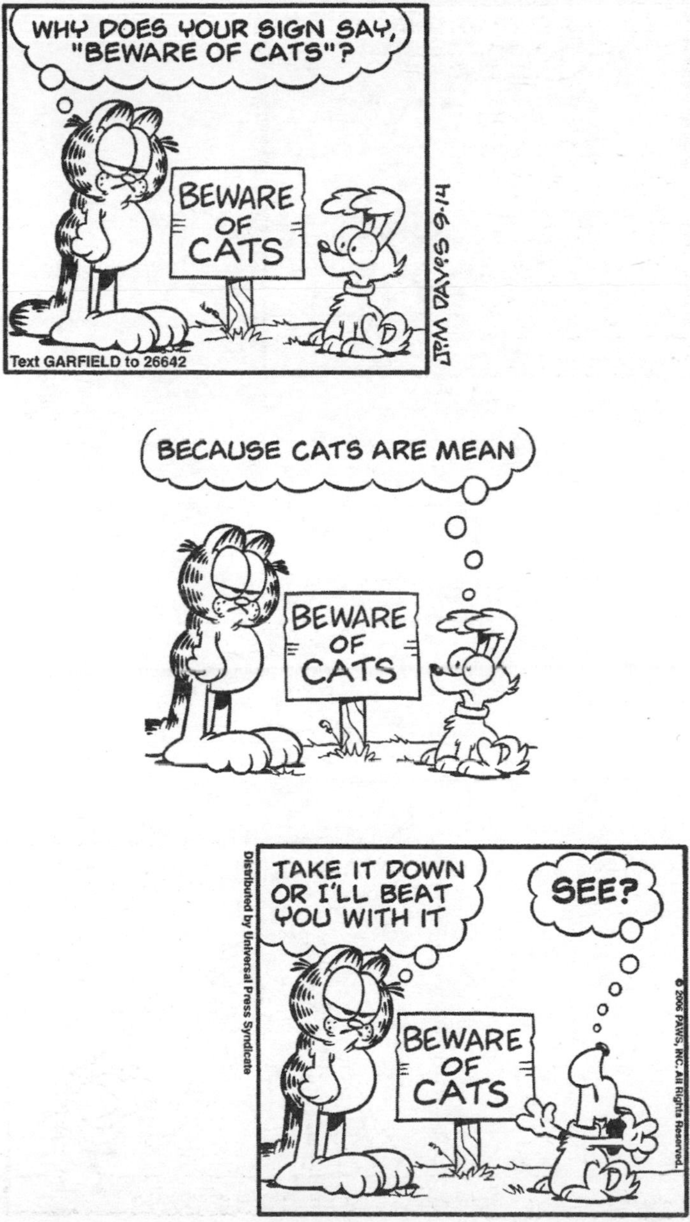
WHY DOES YOUR SIGN SAY, "BEWARE OF CATS"?
BEWARE OF CATS
Text GARFIELD to 26642
JPM DAVIS 9-14
BECAUSE CATS ARE MEAN
BEWARE OF CATS
TAKE IT DOWN OR I'LL BEAT YOU WITH IT
SEE?
BEWARE OF CATS
Distributed by Universal Press Syndicate
© 2006 PAWS, INC. All Rights Reserved.

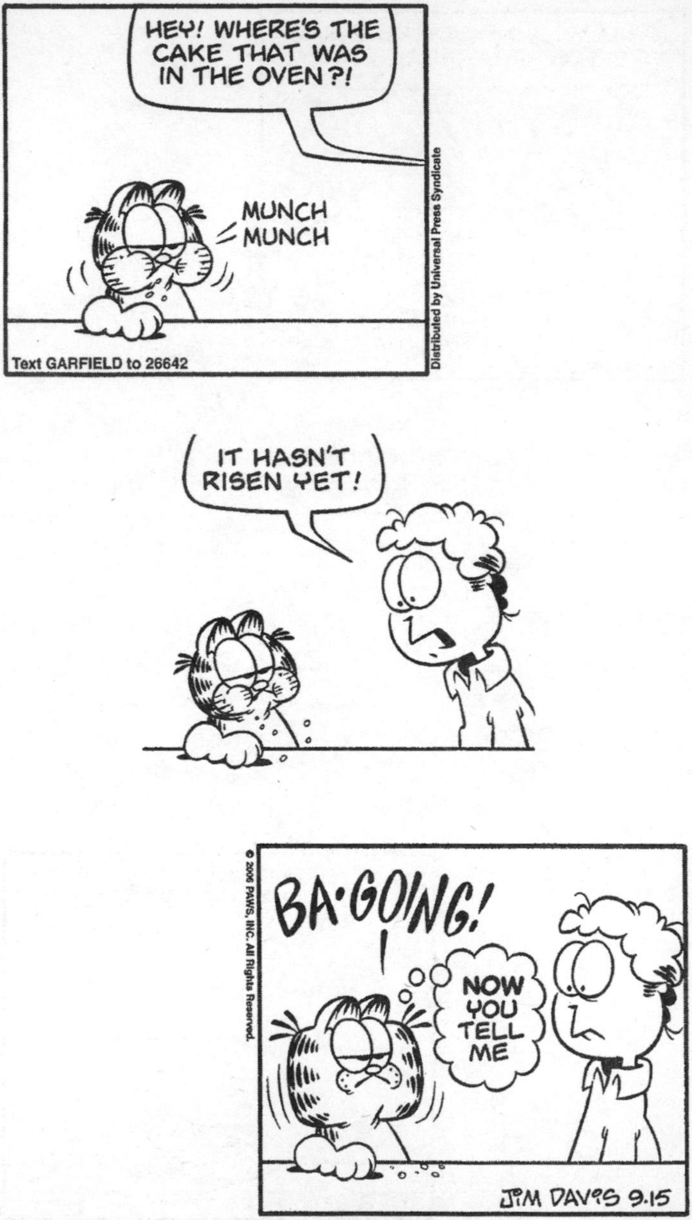
HEY! WHERE'S THE CAKE THAT WAS IN THE OVEN?!
MUNCH MUNCH
Text GARFIELD to 26642
Distributed by Universal Press Syndicate
IT HASN'T RISEN YET!
© 2006 PAWS, INC. All Rights Reserved.
BA·GOING!
NOW YOU TELL ME
JIM DAVIS 9.15

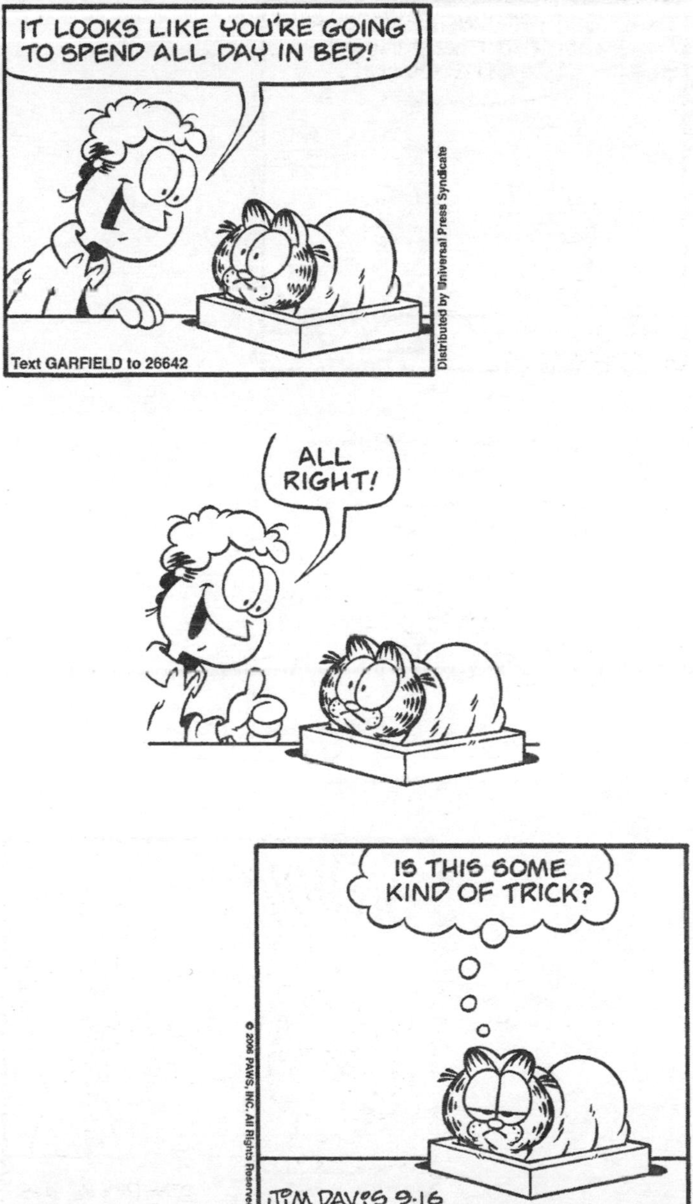
IT LOOKS LIKE YOU'RE GOING TO SPEND ALL DAY IN BED!
Text GARFIELD to 26642
Distributed by Universal Press Syndicate
ALL RIGHT!
IS THIS SOME KIND OF TRICK?
© 2006 PAWS, INC. All Rights Reserved.
JIM DAVIS 9.16

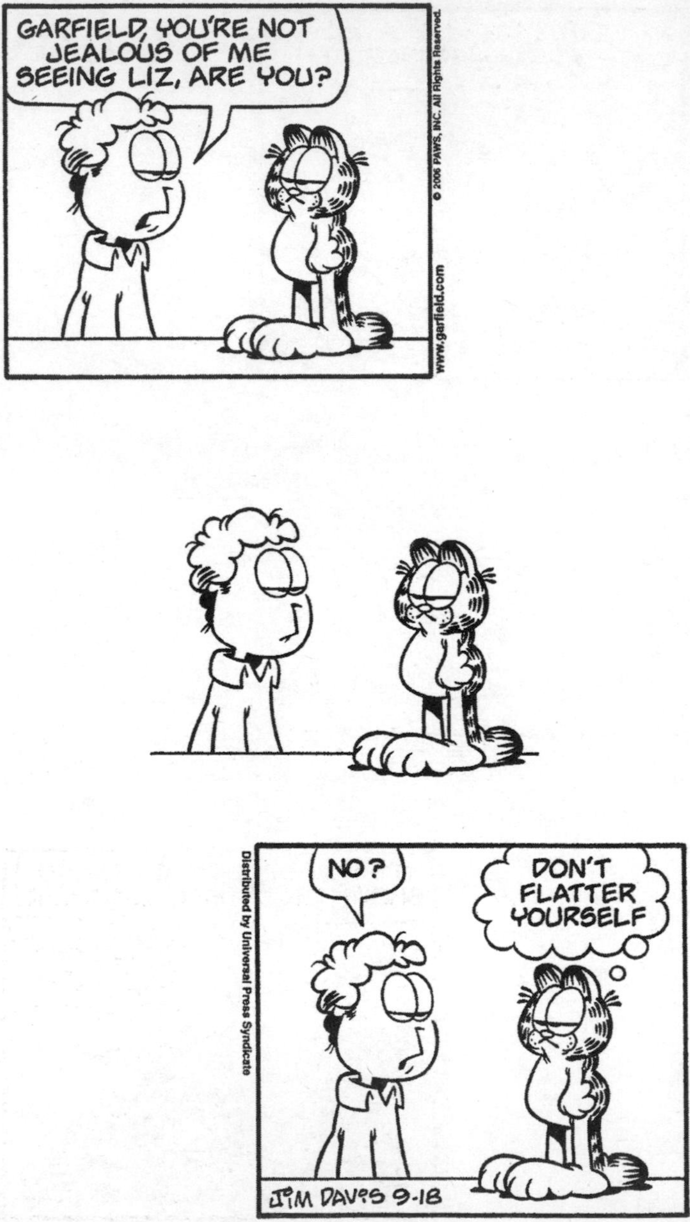
GARFIELD, YOU'RE NOT JEALOUS OF ME SEEING LIZ, ARE YOU?
© 2006 PAWS, INC. All Rights Reserved.
www.garfield.com
Distributed by Universal Press Syndicate
NO?
DON'T FLATTER YOURSELF
JIM DAVIS 9-18

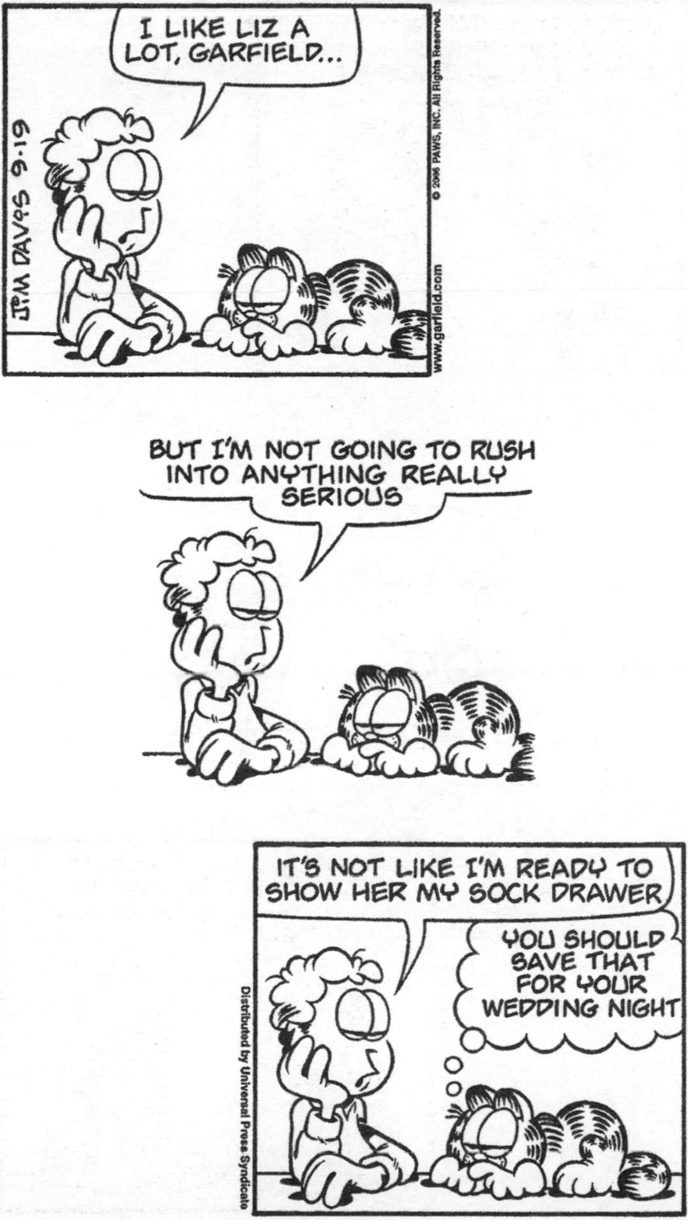
I LIKE LIZ A LOT, GARFIELD...
JIM DAVIS 9·19
© 2006 PAWS, INC. All Rights Reserved.
www.garfield.com
BUT I'M NOT GOING TO RUSH INTO ANYTHING REALLY SERIOUS
IT'S NOT LIKE I'M READY TO SHOW HER MY SOCK DRAWER
YOU SHOULD SAVE THAT FOR YOUR WEDDING NIGHT
Distributed by Universal Press Syndicate

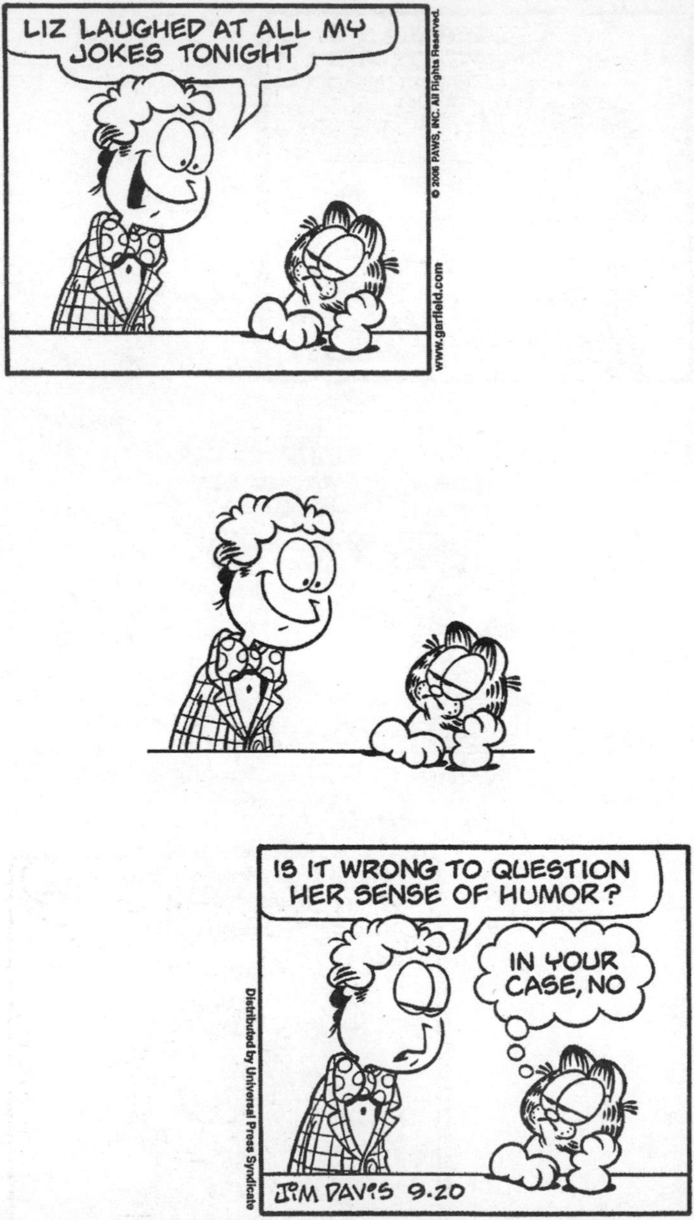
LIZ LAUGHED AT ALL MY JOKES TONIGHT
© 2006 PAWS, INC. All Rights Reserved.
www.garfield.com
IS IT WRONG TO QUESTION HER SENSE OF HUMOR?
IN YOUR CASE, NO
JIM DAVIS 9.20
Distributed by Universal Press Syndicate

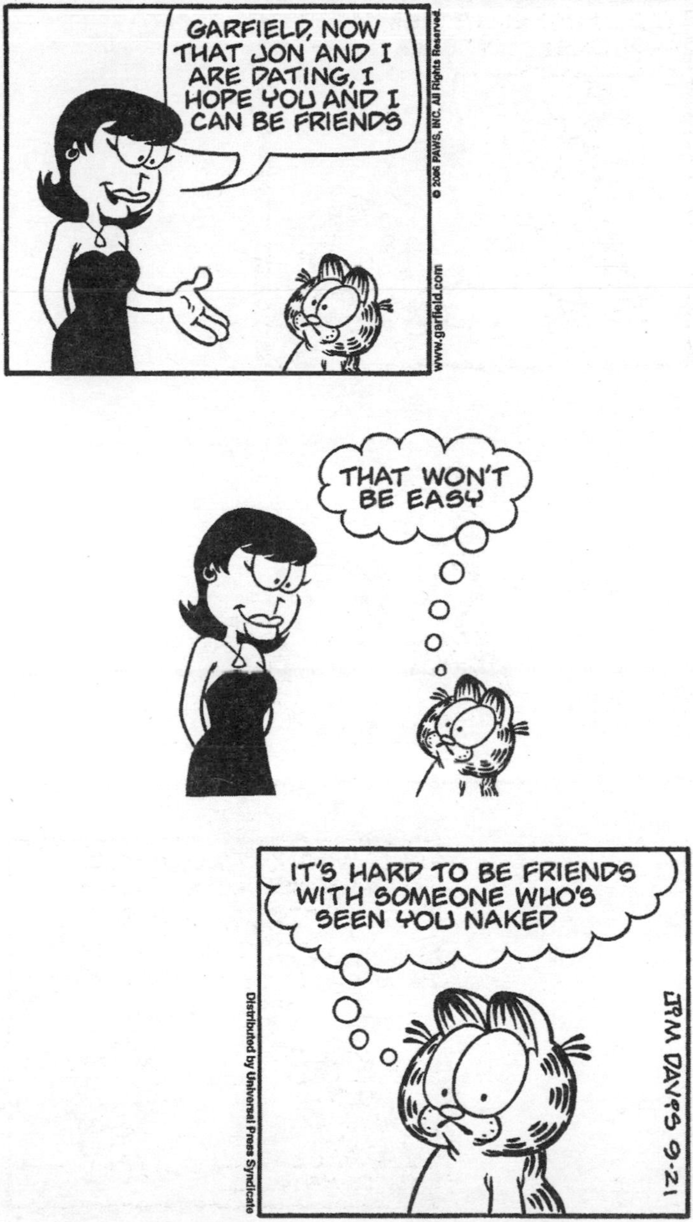
GARFIELD, NOW THAT JON AND I ARE DATING, I HOPE YOU AND I CAN BE FRIENDS
© 2006 PAWS, INC. All Rights Reserved.
www.garfield.com
THAT WON'T BE EASY
IT'S HARD TO BE FRIENDS WITH SOMEONE WHO'S SEEN YOU NAKED
Distributed by Universal Press Syndicate
JIM DAVIS 9-21

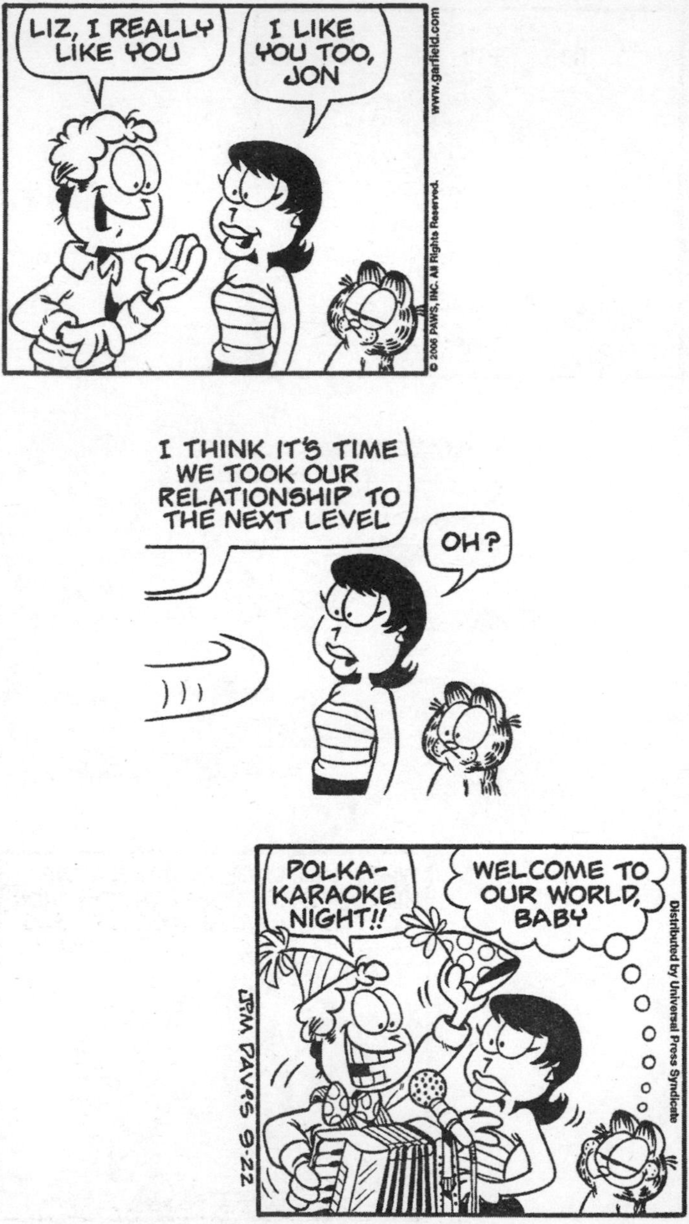
LIZ, I REALLY LIKE YOU
I LIKE YOU TOO, JON
© 2006 PAWS, INC. All Rights Reserved. www.garfield.com
I THINK IT'S TIME WE TOOK OUR RELATIONSHIP TO THE NEXT LEVEL
OH?
POLKA-KARAOKE NIGHT!!
WELCOME TO OUR WORLD, BABY
JIM DAVIS 9-22
Distributed by Universal Press Syndicate

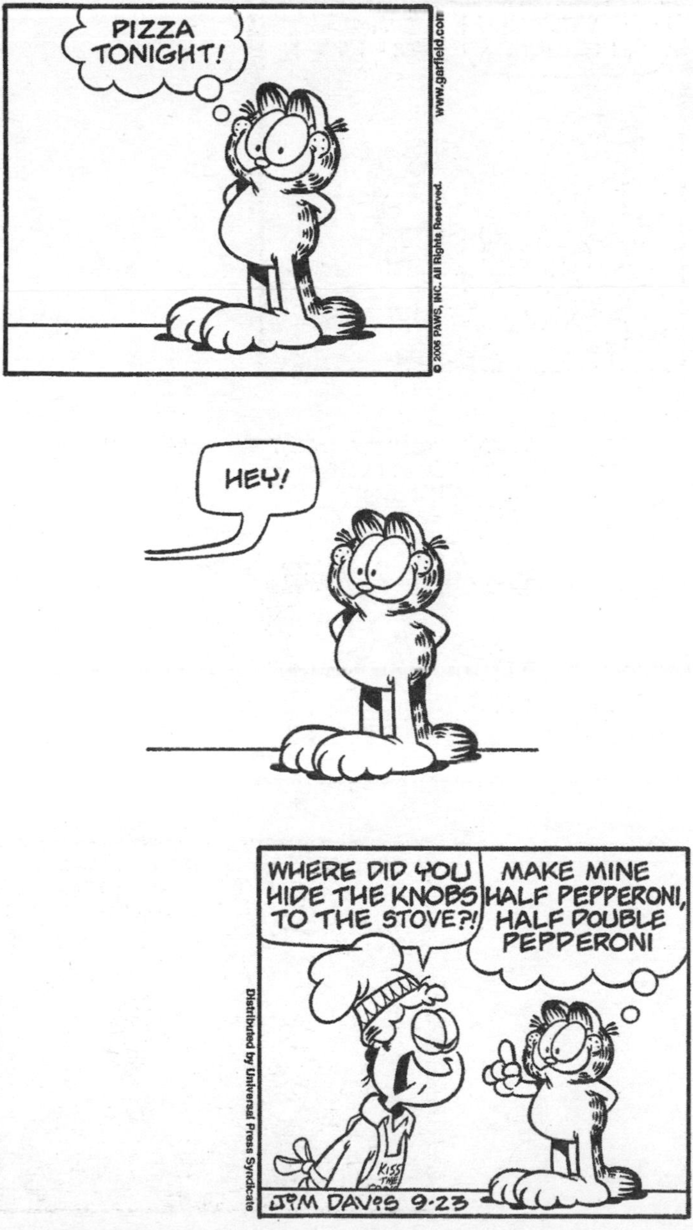
PIZZA TONIGHT!
© 2006 PAWS, INC. All Rights Reserved.
www.garfield.com
HEY!
WHERE DID YOU HIDE THE KNOBS TO THE STOVE?!
MAKE MINE HALF PEPPERONI, HALF DOUBLE PEPPERONI
KISS THE
JIM DAVIS 9-23
Distributed by Universal Press Syndicate

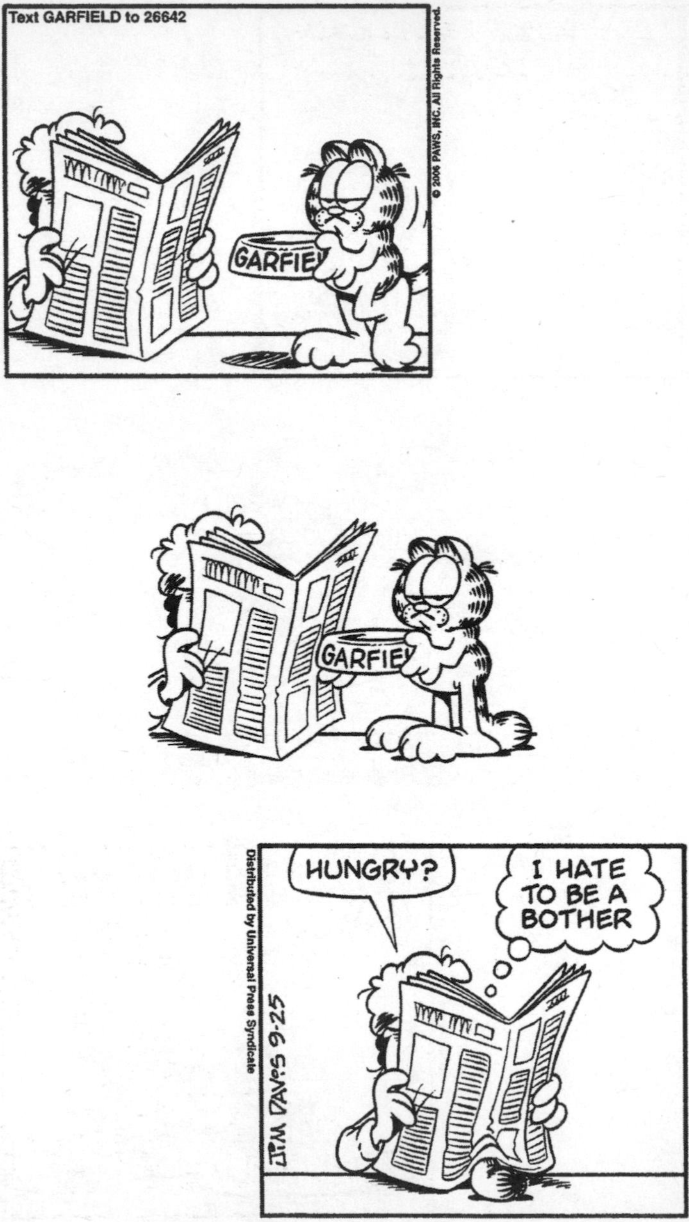
Text GARFIELD to 26642
© 2006 PAWS, INC. All Rights Reserved.
GARFIE
GARFIE
HUNGRY?
I HATE TO BE A BOTHER
JIM DAVIS 9-25
Distributed by Universal Press Syndicate

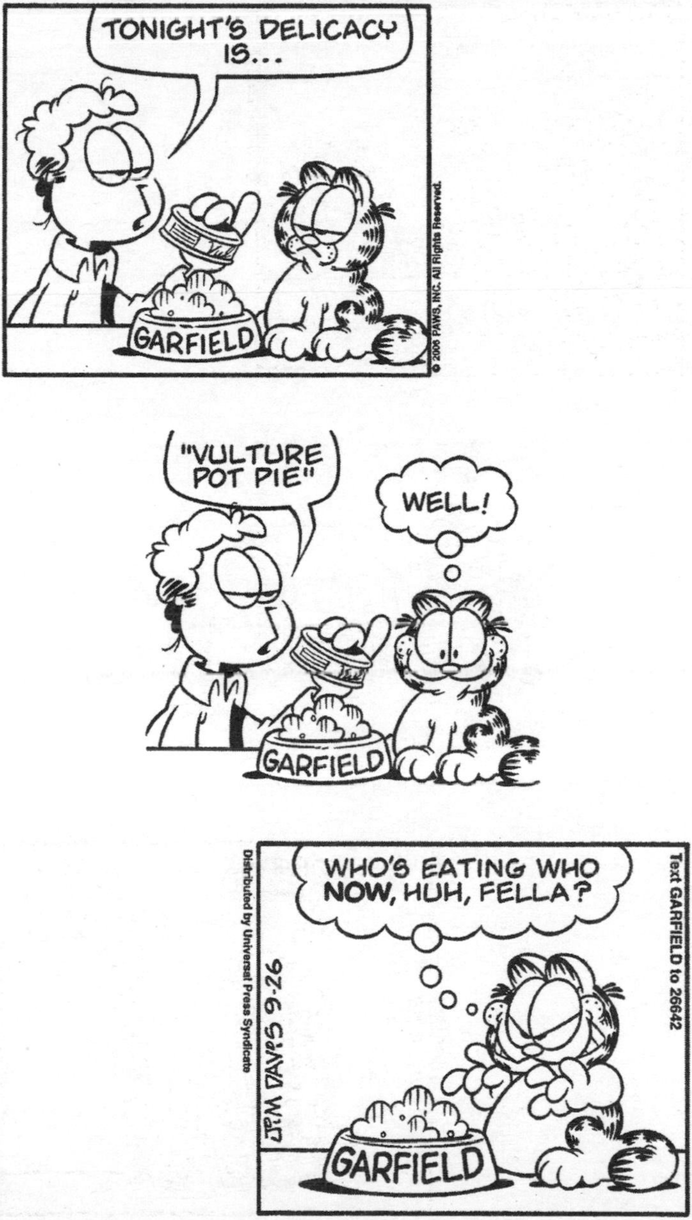
TONIGHT'S DELICACY IS...
GARFIELD
© 2006 PAWS, INC. All Rights Reserved.
"VULTURE POT PIE"
WELL!
GARFIELD
Distributed by Universal Press Syndicate
JIM DAVIS 9-26
WHO'S EATING WHO NOW, HUH, FELLA?
Text GARFIELD to 26642
GARFIELD

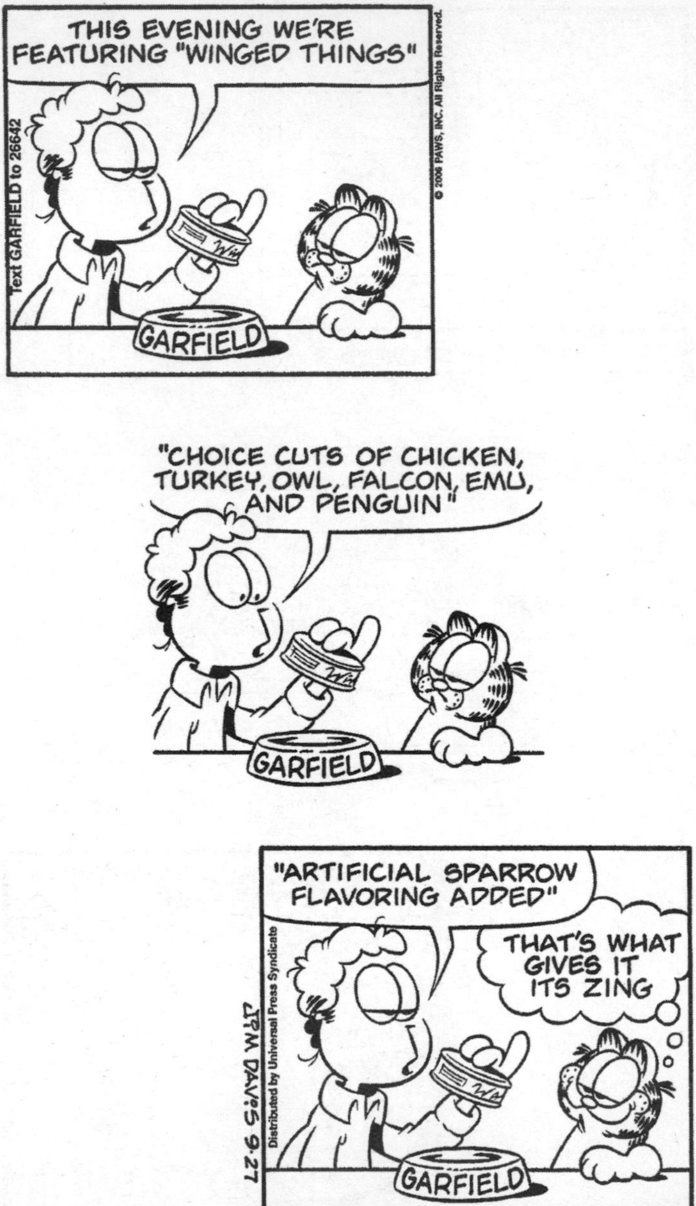
THIS EVENING WE'RE FEATURING "WINGED THINGS"
GARFIELD
Text GARFIELD to 26642
© 2006 PAWS, INC. All Rights Reserved.
"CHOICE CUTS OF CHICKEN, TURKEY, OWL, FALCON, EMU, AND PENGUIN"
GARFIELD
"ARTIFICIAL SPARROW FLAVORING ADDED"
THAT'S WHAT GIVES IT ITS ZING
GARFIELD
Distributed by Universal Press Syndicate
JPM DAVIS 9-27

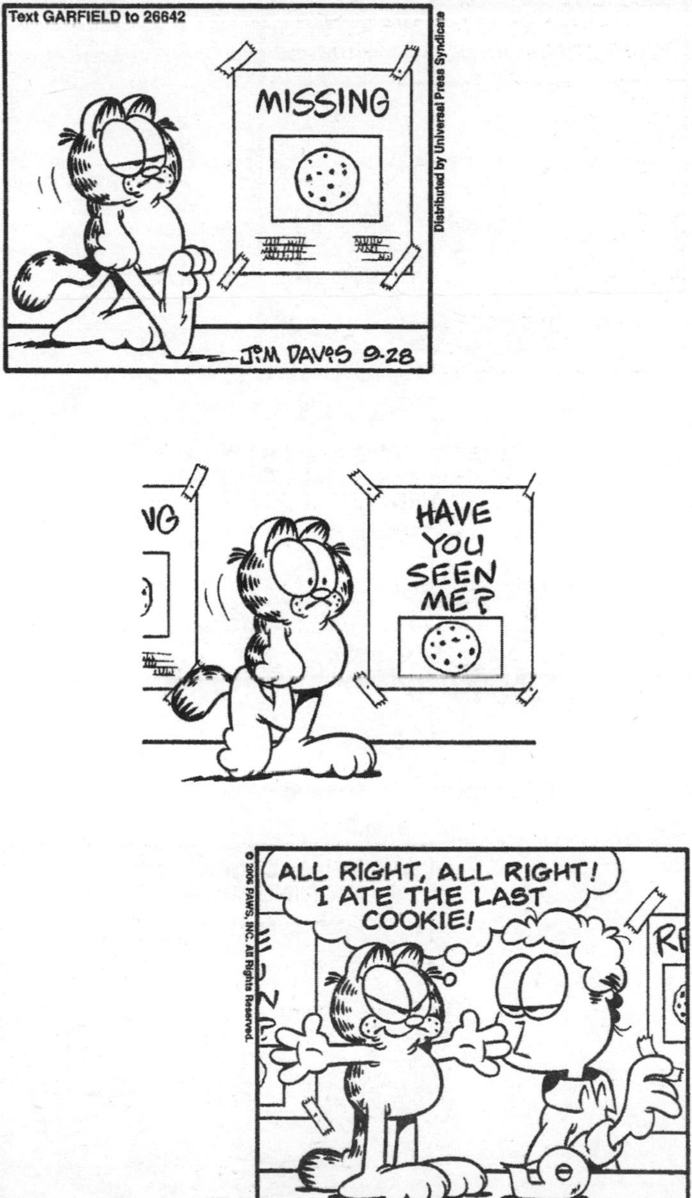

Text GARFIELD to 26642
MISSING
Distributed by Universal Press Syndicate
JIM DAVIS 9-28
HAVE YOU SEEN ME?
ALL RIGHT, ALL RIGHT! I ATE THE LAST COOKIE!
© 2006 PAWS, INC. All Rights Reserved.

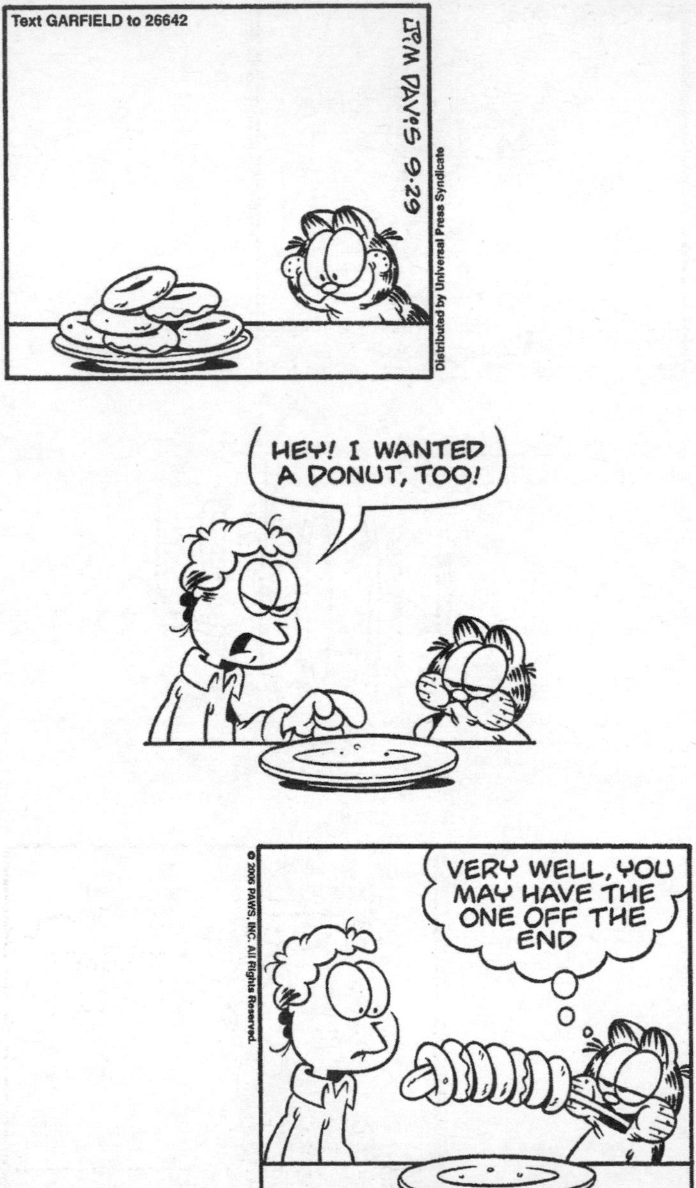
Text GARFIELD to 26642
JIM DAVIS 9·29
Distributed by Universal Press Syndicate
HEY! I WANTED A DONUT, TOO!
© 2006 PAWS, INC. All Rights Reserved.
VERY WELL, YOU MAY HAVE THE ONE OFF THE END

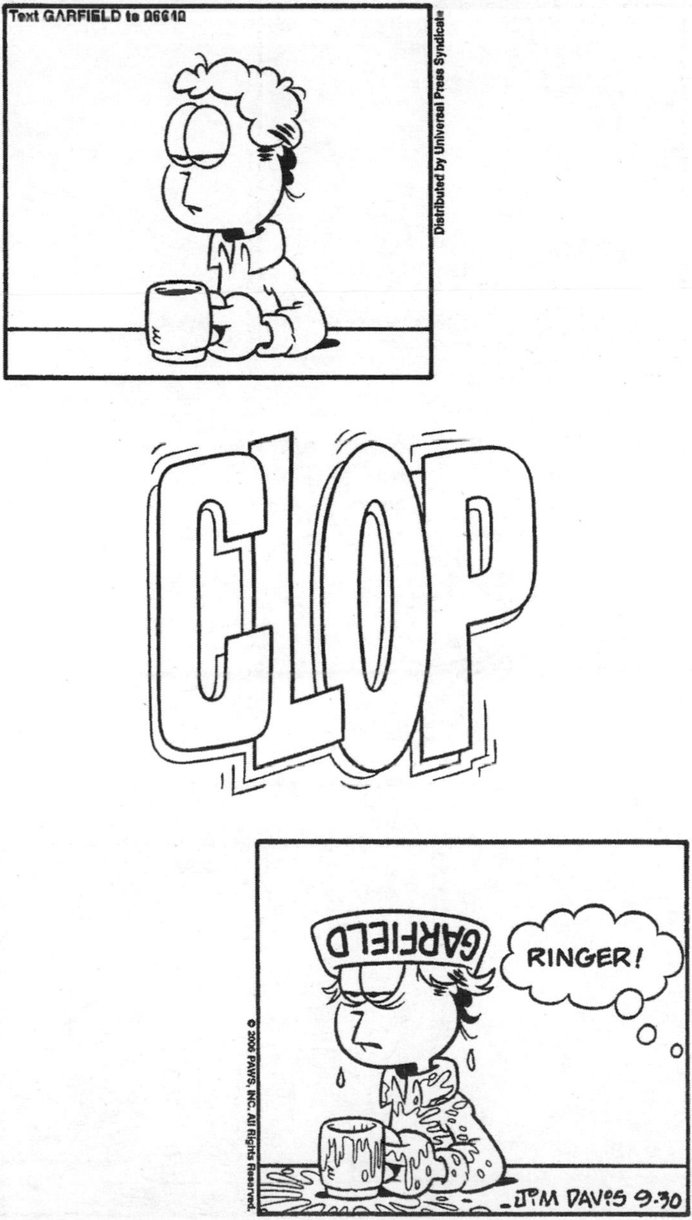
Text GARFIELD to 96610
Distributed by Universal Press Syndicate
CLOP
GARFIELD
RINGER!
© 2006 PAWS, INC. All Rights Reserved.
JIM DAVIS 9-30

HAVING A GIRLFRIEND HAS REALLY OPENED MY EYES, GARFIELD
I'M LEARNING SO MUCH ABOUT WOMEN
SORRY
WELL, I AM!

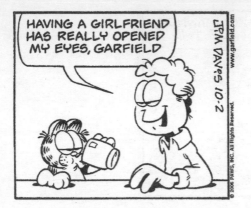

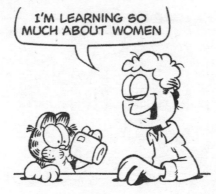

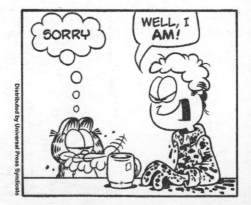

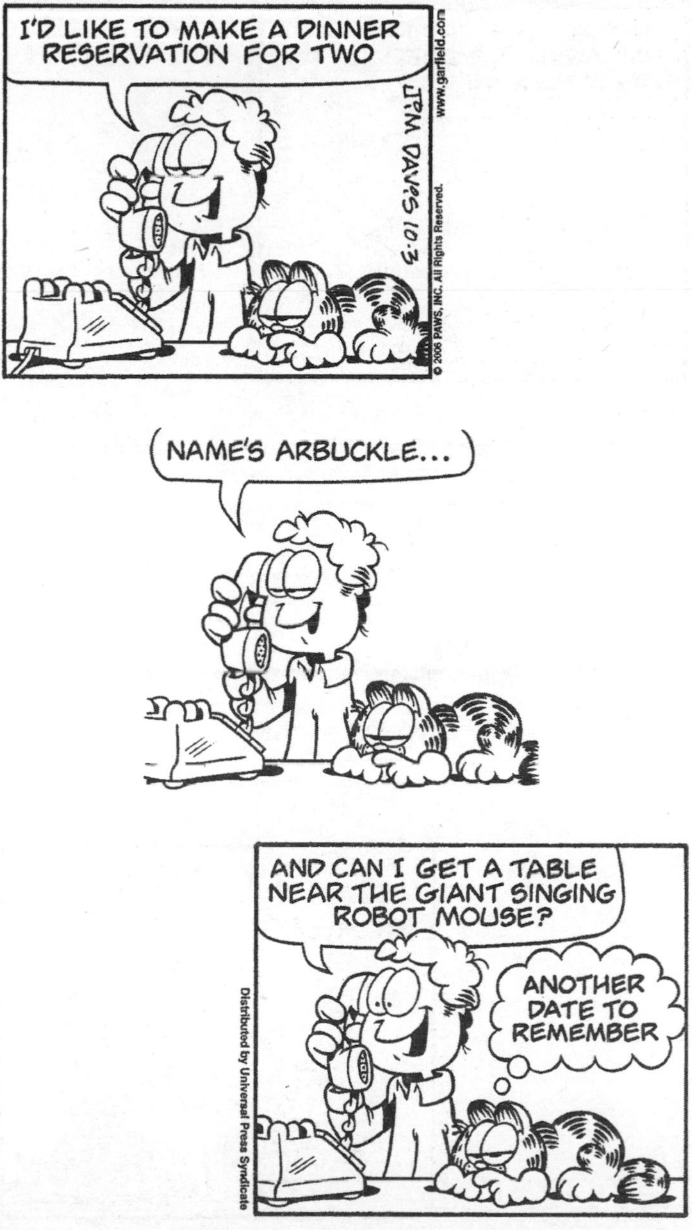
I'D LIKE TO MAKE A DINNER RESERVATION FOR TWO
JIM DAVIS 10·3
© 2006 PAWS, INC. All Rights Reserved.
www.garfield.com
NAME'S ARBUCKLE...
AND CAN I GET A TABLE NEAR THE GIANT SINGING ROBOT MOUSE?
ANOTHER DATE TO REMEMBER
Distributed by Universal Press Syndicate

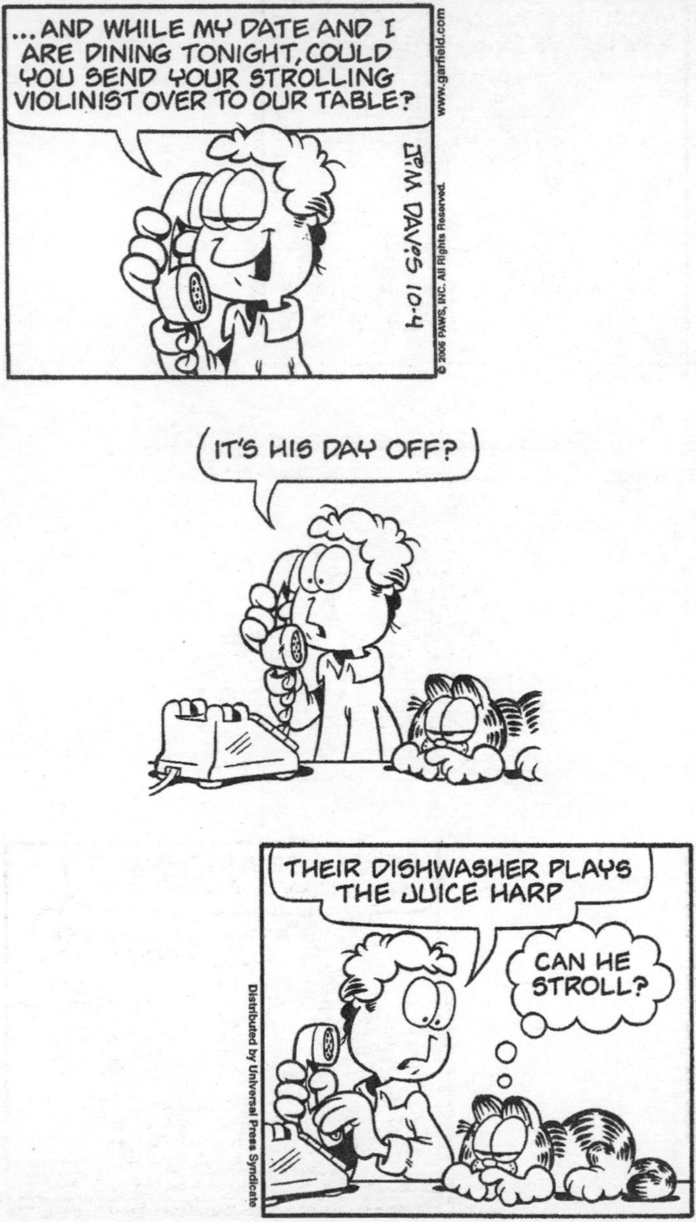
...AND WHILE MY DATE AND I ARE DINING TONIGHT, COULD YOU SEND YOUR STROLLING VIOLINIST OVER TO OUR TABLE?
JIM DAVIS 10-4
www.garfield.com
© 2006 PAWS, INC. All Rights Reserved.
IT'S HIS DAY OFF?
THEIR DISHWASHER PLAYS THE JUICE HARP
CAN HE STROLL?
Distributed by Universal Press Syndicate

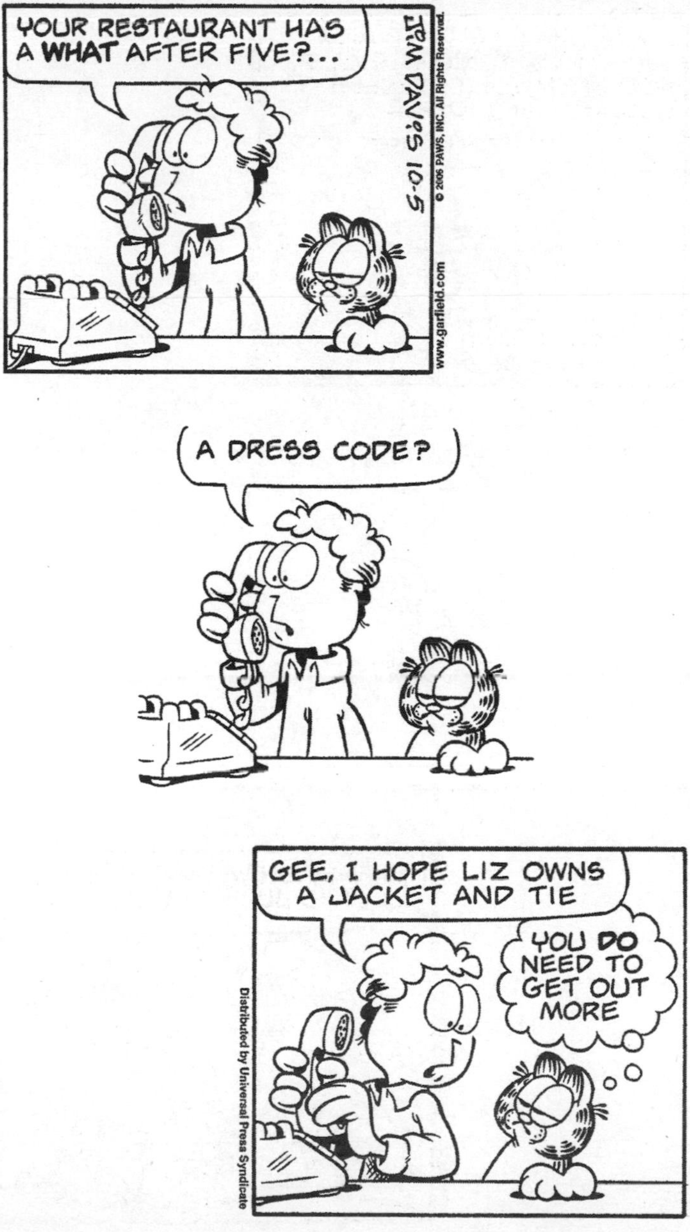
YOUR RESTAURANT HAS A WHAT AFTER FIVE?...
JIM DAVIS 10-5
© 2006 PAWS, INC. All Rights Reserved.
www.garfield.com
A DRESS CODE?
GEE, I HOPE LIZ OWNS A JACKET AND TIE
YOU DO NEED TO GET OUT MORE
Distributed by Universal Press Syndicate

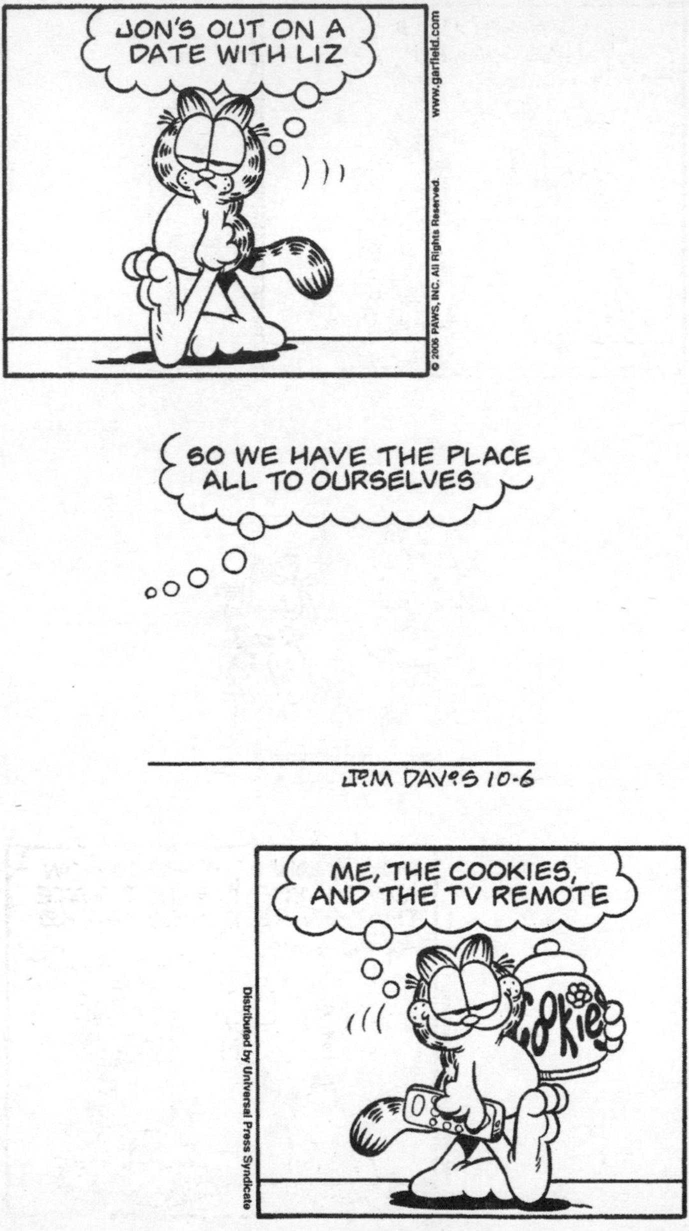
JON'S OUT ON A DATE WITH LIZ
SO WE HAVE THE PLACE ALL TO OURSELVES
ME, THE COOKIES, AND THE TV REMOTE
COOKIES
JIM DAVIS 10-6
© 2006 PAWS, INC. All Rights Reserved. www.garfield.com
Distributed by Universal Press Syndicate

HOW ABOUT A NICE WALK?
www.garfield.com
© 2006 PAWS, INC. All Rights Reserved.
YOU KNOW HOW I HATE THAT STARE
YOU KNOW HOW I HATE NICE WALKS
JIM DAVIS 10-7
Distributed by Universal Press Syndicate

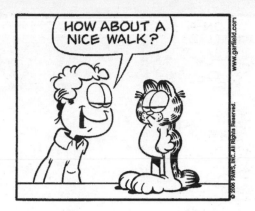

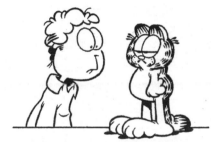

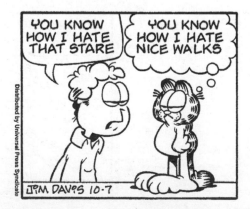

OTHER GARFIELD BOOKS AVAILABLE

Pocket Books		Price	ISBN
Am I Bothered?		£3.99	978-1-84161-286-7
Don't Ask!		£3.99	978-1-84161-247-8
Feed Me!		£3.99	978-1-84161-242-3
Going for Gold		£3.99	978-1-84161-364-2
Gooooal!		£3.99	978-1-84161-329-1
Gotcha!		£3.50	978-1-84161-226-3
I Am What I Am!		£3.99	978-1-84161-243-0
Kowabunga		£3.99	978-1-84161-246-1
Numero Uno		£3.99	978-1-84161-297-3
S.W.A.L.K.		£3.50	978-1-84161-225-6
Talk to the Paw		£3.99	978-1-84161-317-8
Time to Delegate		£3.99	978-1-84161-296-6
Wan2tlk?		£3.99	978-1-84161-264-5
Wassup?		£3.99	978-1-84161-355-0
Whatever!		£3.99	978-1-84161-330-7
Your Point Is?	(new)	£3.99	978-1-84161-370-3

Classics	Price	ISBN
Volume One	£7.99	978-1-85304-970-5
Volume Two	£7.99	978-1-85304-971-2
Volume Three	£7.99	978-1-85304-996-5
Volume Four	£7.99	978-1-85304-997-2
Volume Five	£7.99	978-1-84161-022-1
Volume Six	£7.99	978-1-84161-023-8
Volume Seven	£7.99	978-1-84161-088-7
Volume Eight	£7.99	978-1-84161-089-4
Volume Nine	£7.99	978-1-84161-149-5
Volume Ten	£7.99	978-1-84161-150-1
Volume Eleven	£7.99	978-1-84161-175-4
Volume Twelve	£7.99	978-1-84161-176-1
Volume Thirteen	£7.99	978-1-84161-206-5
Volume Fourteen	£7.99	978-1-84161-207-2
Volume Fifteen	£5.99	978-1-84161-232-4
Volume Sixteen	£5.99	978-1-84161-233-1
Volume Seventeen	£7.99	978-1-84161-250-8
Volume Eighteen	£7.99	978-1-84161 251-5
Volume Nineteen	£7.99	978-1-84161-303-1
Volume Twenty	£6.99	978-1-84161 304-8
Volume Twenty One	£7.99	978-1-84161-359-8

Miscellaneous	Price	ISBN
Colour Collection Book 3	£11.99	978-1-84161-320-8
Colour Collection Book 2	£10.99	978-1-84161-306-2
Garfield & Co (Graphic Novel)	£6.99	978-1-84161-349-9

New Titles
available now

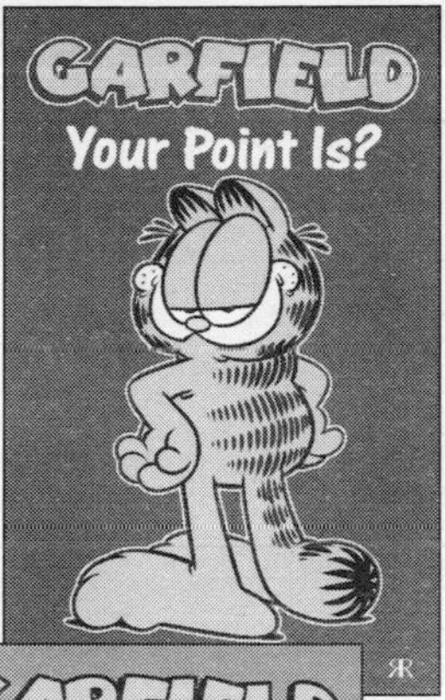
GARFIELD
Your Point Is?

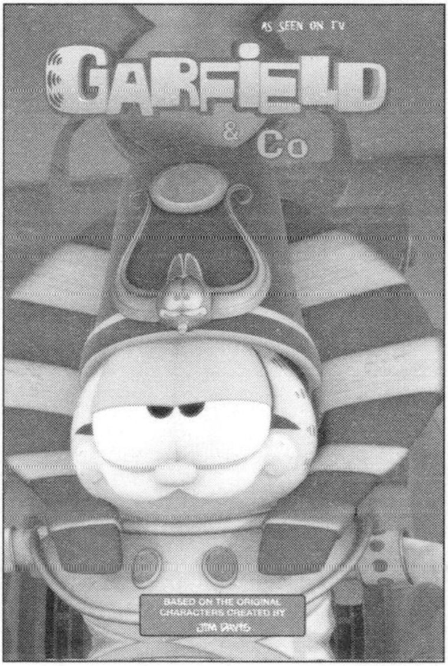
AS SEEN ON TV
GARFIELD
& Co
BASED ON THE ORIGINAL
CHARACTERS CREATED BY
JIM DAVIS

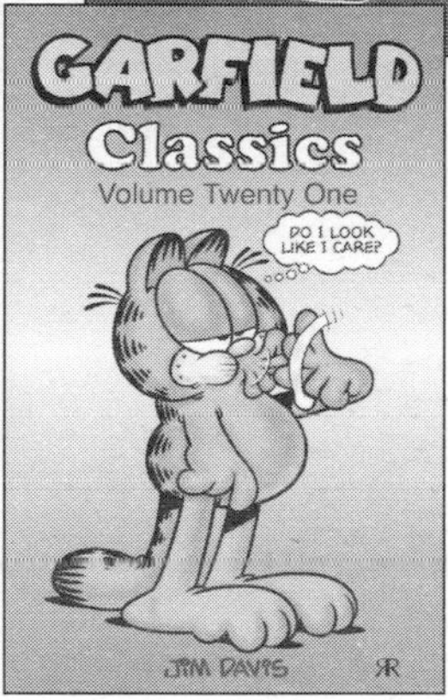
GARFIELD
Classics
Volume Twenty One
DO I LOOK
LIKE I CARE?
JIM DAVIS

All Garfield books are available at your local bookshop
or from the publisher at the address below.

Just send your order with your payment and name and address details to:-

Ravette Publishing Ltd
PO Box 876
Horsham
West Sussex RH12 9GH
(tel: 01403 711443 ... email: ingrid@ravettepub.co.uk)

Prices and availability are subject to change without notice.

Please enclose a cheque or postal order made payable to:
Ravette Publishing to the value of the cover price of the book/s
and allow the following for UK postage and packing:-

70p for the first book + 40p for each additional book
except Colour Collections... when please add £2.00 per book

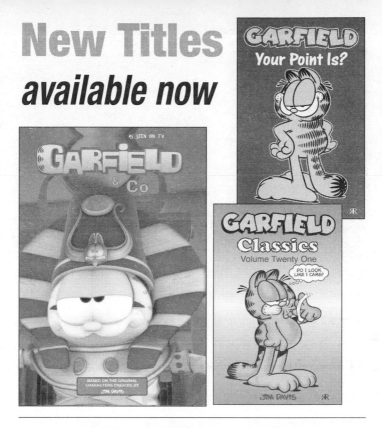